Contents

Introduction to the Student

These *Timed Readings in Literature* are designed to help you become a faster and better reader. As you progress through the book, you will find yourself growing in reading speed and comprehension. You will be challenged to increase your reading rate while maintaining a high level of comprehension.

Reading, like most things, improves with practice. If you practice improving your reading speed, you will improve. As you will see, the rewards of improved reading speed will be well worth your time and effort.

Why Read Faster?

The quick and simple answer is that faster readers are better readers. Does this statement surprise you? You might think that fast readers would miss something and their comprehension might suffer. This is not true, for two reasons:

1. Faster readers comprehend faster. When you read faster, the writer's message is coming to you faster and makes sense sooner. Ideas are interconnected. The writer's thoughts are all tied together, each one leading to the next. The more quickly you can see how ideas are related to each other, the more quickly you can comprehend the meaning of what you are reading.

2. Faster readers concentrate better. Concentration is essential for comprehension. If your mind is wandering you can't understand what you are reading. A lack of concentration causes you to re-read, sometimes over and over, in order to comprehend. Faster readers concentrate better because there's less time for distractions to interfere. Comprehension, in turn, contributes to concentration. If you are concentrating and comprehending, you will not become distracted.

Want to Read More?

Do you wish that you could read more? (or, at least, would you like to do your required reading in less time?) Faster reading will help.

The illustration on the next page shows the number of books someone might read over a period of ten years. Let's see what faster reading could

JAMESTOWN EDUCATION

Titles in This Series
Timed Readings, Third Edition
Timed Readings in Literature

Teaching Notes are available for this text and
will be sent to the instructor. Please write on
school stationery; tell us what grade
you teach and identify the text.

Glencoe/McGraw-Hill
A Division of The McGraw·Hill Companies

Timed Readings in Literature
Book Three

Cover and text design: Deborah Hulsey Christie

ISBN :   0-89061-516-0

Send all Inquiries to:
Glencoe/McGraw-Hill
8787 Orion Place
Columbus, OH 43240-4027

11 12 13 14 021 10 09 08 07 06

JAMESTOWN 🚢 EDUCATION

TIMED READINGS
in Literature
BOOK THREE

Edward Spargo, Editor

Selections & Questions
for this Edition:
Henry Billings
Melissa Billings

Fifty 400-Word Passages
with Questions for
Building Reading Speed

 **Glencoe**
McGraw-Hill

New York, New York   Columbus, Ohio   Chicago, Illinois   Peoria, Illinois   Woodland Hills, California

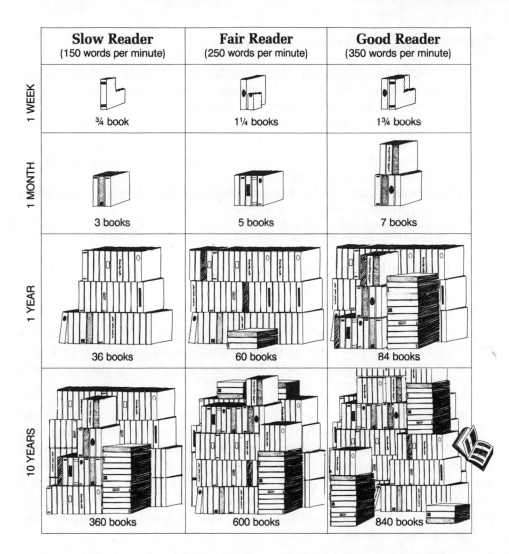

	Slow Reader (150 words per minute)	Fair Reader (250 words per minute)	Good Reader (350 words per minute)
1 WEEK	¾ book	1¼ books	1¾ books
1 MONTH	3 books	5 books	7 books
1 YEAR	36 books	60 books	84 books
10 YEARS	360 books	600 books	840 books

do for you. Look at the stack of books read by a slow reader and the stack read by a good reader. (We show a speed of 350 words a minute for our "good" reader, but many fast readers can more than double that speed.) Let's say, however, that you are now reading at a rate of 150 words a minute. The illustration shows you reading 36 books a year. By increasing your reading speed to 250 words a minute, you could increase the number of books to 60 a year.

We have arrived at these numbers by assuming that the readers in our illustration read for one hour a day, six days a week, and that an average book is about 72,000 words long. Many people do not read that much, but they might if they could learn to read better and faster.

Faster reading doesn't *take* time, it *saves* time!

Acquisitional *vs.* Recreational Reading

Timed Readings in Literature gives practice in a certain kind of reading: recreational reading. Recreational reading of novels and short stories is different from the kind of reading you must employ with textbooks. You read a textbook to *acquire* facts and information. That is acquisitional reading, reading that is careful and deliberate—you cannot afford to miss something you may be quizzed on later. Acquisitional reading speed must be slower than recreational reading speed.

The practice you will be doing in this book will help you develop a high reading speed suitable for literature.

Why Practice on Literature?

If acquisitional reading is so useful and important for students, why should you spend valuable class time learning to read literature faster? Shouldn't you be learning to read textbooks faster and better? Believe it or not, you are! That's right: the reading speed and skills you develop from this book will transfer to your textbooks and to other study reading. Here are some of the ways this happens.

1. The practice effect. In the dictionary, *practice* is defined as systematic exercise to gain proficiency. In other words, repeated drill brings improvement. You know from your own experience that when you practice anything—from piano to basketball—you become better at it. The same holds true for reading. As you are doing the drills and exercises in these books, you are practicing *all* of your reading skills at the same time. With practice you become a fluent reader and comprehender—a better reader of everything you read.

2. Using context. Good readers are aware of context and use it to aid understanding. Context refers to the words surrounding those you are reading. Meaning, you see, does not come from a single word, or even a single sentence—it is conveyed within the whole context of what you are reading.

The language of literature is rich with meaning. The storyteller is trying to *please* the reader, not *teach* the reader. The writer wants to share feelings and experiences with the reader, to reach him or her in a personal way. As you practice reading literature, you are developing your skill in using context to extract the full measure of meaning and appreciation. These same context skills can be put to work when you are reading textbooks to help you organize facts into a meaningful body of knowledge.

3. Vocabulary growth. Our early vocabulary comes from listening—to our families, friends, television, teachers, and classmates. We learn and understand new words as we hear them being used by others. In fact, the more times we encounter a word, the better we understand it. Finally, it becomes ours, part of our permanent vocabulary of words we know and use.

As time goes by, an increasing number of words is introduced to us through recreational reading. Most of the words we know come from reading—words we have never looked up in a dictionary, but whose meanings have become clear to us through seeing them again and again until they are finally ours. Literature, the kind you will be reading in this book, provides countless opportunities for meeting and learning new words. Literature, as you have seen, also provides the context for seeing these new words used with precision and effect. As you work through the pages in this book, you will be developing a larger and stronger vocabulary—a storehouse of words that become your tools for learning.

4. Skills transfer. You are using this book to develop your ability to read literature with increased speed and comprehension. With regular practice and a little effort, you will be successful in reaching that goal.

As we mentioned, you will also be improving your context skills and building a bigger vocabulary. These are all wonderful results from using this book.

But, perhaps the greatest benefit of all is the application of these improvements to all of your reading tasks, not just literature. Using this book will make you a better reader, and *better readers read everything better.*

Reading Literature Faster

Through literature we share an experience with a writer. That experience may be presented as a conversation, a character or scene, an emotion, or an event.

Let's examine these four kinds of presentation. Let's see if there are characteristics or clues we can use to help us identify each kind. Once we know what we are expected to experience, we can read more intelligently and more quickly.

When you are working in this book, your instructor will schedule a few moments for you to preview each selection before timing begins. Use the preview time to scan the selection rapidly, looking for one of the following kinds of presentation.

1. Reading and Understanding a Conversation

A conversation is intended to tell us what characters are thinking or feeling—the best way to do this is through their own words.

Read the following conversation between George and his mother, an excerpt from "George's Mother" by Stephen Crane:

> Finally he said savagely: "Damn these early hours!" His mother jumped as if he had thrown a missile at her. "Why, George—" she began.
>
> George broke in again. "Oh, I know all that—but this gettin' up in th' mornin' so early just makes me sick. Jest when a man is gettin' his mornin' nap he's gotta get up. I—"
>
> "George, dear," said his mother, "yeh know I hate yeh to swear, dear. Now, please don't." She looked beseechingly at him.
>
> He made a swift gesture. "Well, I ain't swearin', am I?" he demanded. "I was only sayin' that this gettin'-up business gives me a pain, wasn't I?"
>
> "Well, yeh know how swearin' hurts me," protested the little old woman. She seemed about to sob. She gazed off . . . apparently recalling persons who had never been profane.

First, is this a conversation? Yes, we know it is. There are quotation marks throughout indicating words spoken by the characters. So, to identify a conversation, we look for quotation marks.

Next, does this conversation tell us what the characters are thinking or feeling? It certainly does—this conversation is unmistakably clear. We know how George *feels* about getting up in the morning, and we know how his mother *feels* about profanity.

Finally, how should we read this and other conversations we encounter in literature? Join the conversation; pretend you are one of the speakers and that these are your own words. Listen to the other character as though words are being addressed to you.

Conversations can be read quickly and understood well when you recognize them and become part of them.

2. Reading About and Understanding a Character or Scene

How do we learn about a character? There are many ways. Writers introduce characters (1) by telling us what they look like; (2) by what they say; (3) by the things they do; and (4) by telling us what others think and say about them:

> He was a staid, placid gentleman, something past the prime of life, yet upright in his carriage for all that, and slim as a greyhound. He was well mounted upon a sturdy chestnut cob, and had the graceful seat of an experienced horseman; while his riding gear, though free from such fopperies as were then in vogue, was handsome and well chosen. He wore a riding coat of a somewhat brighter green than might have been expected to suit the taste of a gentleman of his years, with a short, black velvet cape, and laced pocket holes and cuffs, all of a jaunty fashion; his linen too, was of the finest kind, worked in a rich pattern at the wrists and throat, and scrupulously white. Although he seemed, judging from the mud he had picked up on the way, to have come from London, his horse was as smooth and cool as his own iron-gray periwig and pigtail.

Obviously a character is being introduced to us in this passage from *Barnaby Rudge* by Charles Dickens. We are told how he carries himself and how he is dressed. We even know a little about what he has been doing.

The question to ask yourself is: Is this character lifelike and real? Real characters should be like real people—good and bad, happy and sad, alike and different. In reading about characters, look for the same details you look for in all people.

Similarly, when a scene or location is being described, look for words which tell about size, shape, color, appearance. Such descriptor words help us picture in our minds the place being described. Try to visualize the scene as you read.

3. Experiencing an Emotion Through Literature

When a writer presents an emotion for us to experience, the intent is to produce an effect within us. The intended effect may be pity, fear, revulsion, or some other emotion. The writer wants us to *feel* something.

In the following passage from *Jane Eyre* by Charlotte Brontë, what emotions are we expected to feel for the character?

John had not much affection for his mother and sisters, and an antipathy to me. He bullied and punished me; not two or three times in the week, not once or twice in the day, but continually: every nerve I had feared him, and every morsel of flesh on my bones shrank when he came near. There were moments when I was bewildered by the terror he inspired, because I had no appeal whatever against either his menaces or his inflictions; the servants did not like to offend their young master by taking my part against him, and Mrs. Reed was blind and deaf on the subject: She never saw him strike or heard him abuse me, though he did both now and then in her very presence; more frequently behind her back.

Do you feel sorry for this girl because she is being abused? Do you feel compassion because she is suffering? Are you suffering with her? Do you feel anger toward her abuser? What other effects are intended? How are these effects produced?

Emotional and provocative words and expressions have been employed by the writer to paint a vivid portrait of her character's predicament. Can you identify some of the words? What did John do? He *bullied*, *struck*, *punished*, and *abused*. The girl felt fear, bewilderment, and terror. These very expressive and emotional words and phrases are the clues provided by the writer to help her readers read and comprehend effectively.

4. Reading About and Understanding an Event

In describing an event—a series of actions—the writer is telling us a story, and the elements of the story are presented in some kind of order or pattern. Read this passage from *Around the World in Eighty Days* by Jules Verne:

Mr. Fogg and his two companions took their places on a bench opposite the desks of the magistrate and his clerk. Immediately after, Judge Obadiah, a fat, round man, followed by the clerk, entered. He proceeded to take down a wig which was hanging on a nail, and put it hurriedly on his head.

"The first case," said he. Then, putting his hand to his head, he exclaimed "Heh! This is not my wig!"

"No, your worship," returned the clerk, "it is mine."

"My dear Mr. Oysterpuff, how can a judge give a wise sentence in a clerk's wig?"

The wigs were exchanged.

Did you see how this little story was told? The events in the story were presented in chronological order—from first to last as they occurred. This is a frequently used and easily recognized pattern, but not the only one writers use. The story could have been told in reverse—the story could have opened with the judge wearing the wrong wig and then gone on to explain how the mistake happened.

In passages like these, look for the events in the story and see how they are related, how one event follows or builds on the other. By recognizing the pattern of storytelling and using the pattern as an aid to organizing and understanding the events, you can become a better and faster reader.

How to Use This Book

Reading Literature Faster

Through literature we share an experience with a writer. That experience may be presented as a conversation, a character or scene, an emotion, or an event.

Let's examine these four kinds of presentation. Let's see if there are characteristics or clues we can use to help us identify each kind. Once we know what we are expected to experience, we can read more intelligently and more quickly.

When you are working in this book, your instructor will schedule a few moments for you to preview each selection before timing begins. Use the preview time to scan the selection rapidly, looking for one of the following kinds of presentation.

1. Reading and Understanding a Conversation

A conversation is intended to tell us what characters are thinking or feeling—the best way to do this is through their own words.

Read the following conversation between George and his mother, an excerpt from "George's Mother" by Stephen Crane.

1 Read the lessons

First, read the lessons on pages 8 through 11. These lessons teach you how to recognize and identify the kinds of presentation you encounter in literature and in the selections in this book.

2 Preview

Find a literature selection to read and wait for your instructor's signal to preview. You will have 30 seconds to preview (scan) the selection to identify the author's kind of presentation.

3 Begin reading

When your instructor gives you the signal, begin reading. Read at a slightly faster-than-normal speed. Read well enough so that you will be able to answer questions about what you have read.

7 Fill in the progress graph

Enter your score and plot your reading time on the graph on page 118 or 119. The right-hand side of the graph shows your words-per-minute reading speed. Write this number at the bottom of the page on the line labeled *Words per Minute*.

4 Record your time

When you finish reading, look at the blackboard and note your reading time. Your reading time will be the lowest time remaining on the board, or the next number to be erased. Write this time at the bottom of the page on the line labeled *Reading Time*.

5 Answer the questions

Answer the ten questions on the next page. There are five fact questions and five thought questions. Pick the *best* answer to each question and put an x in the box beside it.

6 Correct your answers

Using the Answer Key on pages 116 and 117, correct your work. Circle your wrong answers and put an x in the box you should have marked. Score 10 points for each correct answer. Write your score at the bottom of the page on the line labeled *Comprehension Score*.

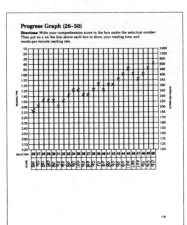

Progress Graph (26–50)
Directions: Write your comprehension score in the box under the selection number. Then put an x on the line above each box to show your reading time and words-per-minute reading rate.

Instructions for the Pacing Drills

From time to time your instructor may wish to conduct pacing drills using *Timed Readings*. For this work you need to use the Pacing Dots printed in the margins of your book pages. The dots will help you regulate your reading speed to match the pace set by your instructor or announced on the reading cassette tape.

Pacing Dots

You will be reading at the correct pace if you are at the dot when your instructor says "Mark" or when you hear a tone on the tape. If you are ahead of the pace, read a little more slowly; if you are behind the pace, increase your reading speed. Try to match the pace exactly.

Follow these steps.

Step 1: Record the pace. At the bottom of the page, write on the line labeled *Words per Minute* the rate announced by the instructor or by the speaker on the tape.

Step 2: Begin reading. Wait for the signal to begin reading. Read at a slightly faster-than-normal speed. You will not know how on-target your pace is until you hear your instructor say "Mark" or until you hear the first tone on the tape. After a little practice you will be able to select an appropriate starting speed most of the time.

Step 3: Adjust your pace. As you read, try to match the pace set by the instructor or the tape. Read more slowly or more quickly as necessary. You should be reading the line beside the dot when you hear the pacing signal. The pacing sounds may distract you at first. Don't worry about it. Keep reading and your concentration will return.

Step 4: Stop and answer questions. Stop reading when you are told to, even if you have not finished the selection. Answer the questions right away. Correct your work and record your score on the line *Comprehension Score*. Strive to maintain 80 percent comprehension on each drill as you gradually increase your pace.

Step 5: Fill in the pacing graph. Transfer your words-per-minute rate to the box labeled *Pace* on the pacing graph on page 120. Then plot your comprehension score on the line above the box.

These pacing drills are designed to help you become a more flexible reader. They encourage you to "break out" of a pattern of reading everything at the same speed.

The drills help in other ways, too. Sometimes in a reading program you reach a certain level and bog down. You don't seem able to move on and progress. The pacing drills will help you to work your way out of such slumps and get your reading program moving again.

It is a truth universally acknowledged that a single man in possession of a good fortune must be in want of a wife. However little known the feelings or views of such a man may be on his first entering a neighborhood, this truth is so well fixed in the minds of the surrounding families, that he is considered as the rightful property of some or other of their daughters.

"My dear Mr. Bennet," said his lady to him one day, "have you heard that Netherfield Park is let at last?"

Mr. Bennet replied that he had not.

"But it is," returned she, "for Mrs. Long told me all about it."

Mr. Bennet made no answer.

"Do not you want to know who has taken it?" cried his wife, impatiently.

"You want to tell me, and I have no objection to hearing it."

This was invitation enough.

"Why, my dear, you must know, Mrs. Long says that Netherfield is taken by a young man of large fortune from the north of England; that he came down on Monday in a chaise-and-four to see the place, and was so much delighted with it that he agreed with Mr. Morris immediately; that he is to take possession before Michaelmas, and some of his servants are to be in the house by the end of next week."

"What is his name?"

"Bingley."

"Is he married or single?"

"Oh, single, my dear, to be sure!" A single man of large fortune—four or five thousand a year. What a fine thing for our girls!"

"How so? How can it affect them?"

"My dear Mr. Bennet," replied his wife, "how can you be so tiresome? You must know that I am thinking of his marrying one of them."

"Is that his design in settling here?"

"Design? Nonsense, how can you talk so! But it is very likely that he may fall in love with one of them, and therefore you must visit him as soon as he comes."

"I see no occasion for that. You and the girls may go, or you may send them by themselves, which perhaps will be still better; for as you are as handsome as any of them, Mr. Bingley might like you the best of the party."

"My dear, you flatter me. I certainly have had my share of beauty, but I do not pretend to be anything extraordinary now."

Recalling Facts

1. The young man came from the
   - ☐ a. coast of Ireland.
   - ☐ b. north of England.
   - ☐ c. south of Scotland.

2. The young man made a rental agreement with
   - ☐ a. Mr. Morris.
   - ☐ b. Mrs. Long.
   - ☐ c. Mr. Bennet.

3. The young man was to take possession of Netherfield Park before
   - ☐ a. Easter.
   - ☐ b. Christmas.
   - ☐ c. Michaelmas.

4. Mrs. Bennet wanted Bingley to
   - ☐ a. marry one of her daughters.
   - ☐ b. settle somewhere else.
   - ☐ c. fall in love with her.

5. Mrs. Bennet admitted that she was once
   - ☐ a. not inclined to arrange marriages.
   - ☐ b. a neighbor of Bingley.
   - ☐ c. more beautiful than now.

Understanding the Passage

6. The belief of most people seems to be that a single man
   - ☐ a. needs a wife.
   - ☐ b. should make his fortune first.
   - ☐ c. should run for public office.

7. Netherfield Park appears to be
   - ☐ a. a town.
   - ☐ b. a city park.
   - ☐ c. an estate.

8. Mr. Bennet did not share his wife's enthusiasm for
   - ☐ a. his daughters.
   - ☐ b. visiting Bingley.
   - ☐ c. the approval of their neighbors.

9. Mr. Bennet thought his wife was
   - ☐ a. very intelligent.
   - ☐ b. aging rapidly.
   - ☐ c. still attractive.

10. Mr. Bennet thought his wife was being
   - ☐ a. reasonable.
   - ☐ b. a bit too aggressive.
   - ☐ c. unnecessarily cautious.

from **The Red Badge of Courage** *by Stephen Crane*

The advance of the enemy had seemed to the youth like a ruthless hunting. He began to fume with rage and exasperation. He scowled with hate at the swirling smoke that was approaching like a phantom flood. There was a maddening quality in this seeming resolution of the foe to give him no rest, to give him no time to sit down and think. Yesterday he had fought and had fled rapidly. For today he felt that he had earned opportunities for contemplative repose. He could have enjoyed portraying to uninitiated listeners various scenes at which he had been a witness or ably discussing the processes of war with other proved men. Too it was important that he should have time for physical healing. He was sore and stiff from his experiences. He had received his fill of all exertions, and he wished to rest.

But those other men seemed never to grow weary. They were fighting with their old speed. He had a wild hate for the relentless foe. Yesterday, when he had imagined the universe to be against him, he had hated it, little gods and big gods; today he hated the army of the foe with the same great hatred. He was not going to be badgered of his life, like a kitten chased by boys, he said. It was not well to drive men into final corners; at those moments they could all develop teeth and claws.

He leaned and spoke into his friend's ear. He menaced the woods with a gesture. "If they keep on chasing us, by Gawd, they'd better watch out. Can't stand *too* much."

The friend twisted his head and made a calm reply. "If they keep on a-chasing us they'll drive us all into the river."

The youth cried out savagely at this statement. He crouched behind a little tree, with his eyes burning hatefully and his teeth set in a curlike snarl. The awkward bandage was still about his head, and upon it, over his wound, there was a spot of dry blood. His hair was wondrously tousled, and some straggling, moving locks hung over the cloth of the bandage down toward his forehead. His jacket and shirt were open at the throat, and exposed his young bronzed neck. There could be seen spasmodic gulpings at his throat. His fingers twined nervously about his rifle.

Recalling Facts

1. The enemy was
   - ☐ a. advancing.
   - ☐ b. retreating.
   - ☐ c. not moving.

2. Yesterday the youth had
   - ☐ a. fought in a battle.
   - ☐ b. enlisted in the army.
   - ☐ c. marched through flooded fields.

3. On this day the youth directed his hatred toward
   - ☐ a. his fellow soldiers.
   - ☐ b. the army of the foe.
   - ☐ c. the universe.

4. On his head the youth had a
   - ☐ a. hat.
   - ☐ b. bandage.
   - ☐ c. bronze star.

5. The youth crouched behind
   - ☐ a. his friend.
   - ☐ b. a small tree.
   - ☐ c. a stone wall.

Understanding the Passage

6. The youth desperately wanted to
   - ☐ a. attack the enemy again.
   - ☐ b. rest his mind and body.
   - ☐ c. make it to the river.

7. The enemy showed no signs of
   - ☐ a. making any progress.
   - ☐ b. slowing down.
   - ☐ c. bravery or courage.

8. The youth's friend feared the enemy might
   - ☐ a. kill their leader.
   - ☐ b. drive them back to the river.
   - ☐ c. take them prisoner.

9. The youth had evidently been
   - ☐ a. taken prisoner twice before.
   - ☐ b. involved in knife fights.
   - ☐ c. wounded in battle.

10. The youth's attitude could best be described as
   - ☐ a. scared but defiant.
   - ☐ b. meek and retiring.
   - ☐ c. fearless and bold.

3   *from* **Uncle Tom's Cabin** *by Harriet Beecher Stowe*

Mrs. Shelby had gone on her visit, and Eliza stood on the verandah, rather dejectedly looking after the retreating carriage, when a hand was laid on her shoulder. She turned, and a bright smile lighted up her fine eyes.

"George, is it you? How you frightened me! Well, I'm so glad you've come! Missis is gone to spend the afternoon; so come into my little room, and we'll have the time all to ourselves." Saying this, she drew him into a neat little apartment opening on the verandah, where she generally sat at her sewing, within call of her mistress.

"How glad I am!—why don't you smile?—and look at Harry—how he grows." The boy stood shyly regarding his father through his curls, holding close to the skirts of his mother's dress. "Isn't he beautiful?" said Eliza, lifting his long curls and kissing him.

"I wish he'd never been born," said George, bitterly. "I wish I'd never been born myself!"

Surprised and frightened, Eliza sat down, leaned her head on her husband's shoulder, and burst into tears.

"There now, Eliza, it's too bad for me to make you feel so, poor girl!" said he, fondly; "it's too bad. Oh, how I wish you never had seen me—you might have been happy."

"George! George! how can you talk so? What dreadful thing has happened, or is going to happen? I'm sure we've been very happy till lately."

"So we have, dear," said George. Then drawing his child on his knee, he gazed intently on his glorious dark eyes, and passed his hands through his long curls. "Just like you, Eliza; and you are the handsomest woman I ever saw, and the best one I ever wish to see; but, oh, I wish I'd never seen you, nor you me!"

"Oh, George! how can you?"

"Yes, Eliza, it's all misery, misery, misery! My life is bitter as wormwood; the very life is burning out of me. I'm a poor, miserable, forlorn drudge; I shall only drag you down with me, that's all. What's the use of our trying to do anything, trying to know anything, trying to be anything? What's the use of living? I wish I was dead!"

"Oh, now, dear George, that is really wicked! I know how you feel about losing your place in the factory, and you have a hard master; but pray be patient."

Recalling Facts

1. George was Eliza's
   - ☐ a. master.
   - ☐ b. husband.
   - ☐ c. son.

2. Mrs. Shelby planned to be gone
   - ☐ a. for the afternoon.
   - ☐ b. all day.
   - ☐ c. for the weekend.

3. Harry was George's
   - ☐ a. brother.
   - ☐ b. nephew.
   - ☐ c. son.

4. Harry had
   - ☐ a. blue eyes.
   - ☐ b. long curls.
   - ☐ c. both a and b.

5. George had just lost his job in the
   - ☐ a. field.
   - ☐ b. kitchen.
   - ☐ c. factory.

Understanding the Passage

6. When Eliza first saw George on the verandah, she
   - ☐ a. was happy to see him.
   - ☐ b. immediately began to cry.
   - ☐ c. tried to stop Mrs. Shelby's carriage.

7. Eliza was especially proud of her
   - ☐ a. sewing.
   - ☐ b. master.
   - ☐ c. son.

8. George
   - ☐ a. loved Eliza.
   - ☐ b. hated Eliza.
   - ☐ c. mostly ignored Eliza.

9. George felt that
   - ☐ a. his life was ruined.
   - ☐ b. it was time for him to move on.
   - ☐ c. he had to divorce Eliza.

10. Eliza was
    - ☐ a. saddened by her husband's appearance.
    - ☐ b. concerned about her husband's mood.
    - ☐ c. upset over her husband's rare visits.

When their mutual labor was all finished, Hepzibah took Phoebe's hand in her own trembling one.

"Bear with me, my dear child," she cried; "for truly my heart is full to the brim! Bear with me; for I love you, Phoebe, though I speak so roughly! Think nothing of it, dearest child! By and by, I shall be kind, and only kind!"

"My dearest cousin, cannot you tell me what has happened?" asked Phoebe, with a sunny and tearful sympathy. "What is it that moves you so?"

"Hush! hush! He is coming!" whispered Hepzibah, hastily wiping her eyes. "Let him see you first, Phoebe; for you are young and rosy, and cannot help letting a smile break out whether or no. He always liked bright faces! And mine is old now, and the tears are hardly dry on it. He never could abide tears. There—draw the curtain a little, so that the shadow may fall across his side of the table! But let there be a good deal of sunshine, too; for he never was fond of gloom, as some people are. He has had but little sunshine in his life—poor Clifford—and, oh, what a black shadow! Poor, poor Clifford!"

Thus murmuring in an undertone, as if speaking rather to her own heart than to Phoebe, the old gentlewoman stepped on tiptoe about the room, making such arrangements as suggested themselves at the crisis.

Meanwhile there was a step in the passageway, above stairs. Phoebe recognized it as the same which had passed upward, as through her dream, in the nighttime. The approaching guest, whoever it might be, appeared to pause at the head of the staircase. He paused twice or thrice in the descent. He paused again at the foot. Each time, the delay seemed to be without purpose. Finally, he made a long pause at the threshold of the parlor. He took hold of the knob of the door, then loosened his grasp without opening it. Hepzibah, her hands convulsively clasped, stood gazing at the entrance.

"Dear Cousin Hepzibah, pray don't look so!" said Phoebe, trembling; for her cousin's emotions, and this mysteriously reluctant step, made her feel as if a ghost were coming into the room. "You really frighten me! Is something awful going to happen?"

"Hush!" whispered Hepzibah. "Be cheerful! Whatever may happen, be nothing but cheerful!"

Recalling Facts

1. Phoebe was
   - ☐ a. old and tearful.
   - ☐ b. young and rosy.
   - ☐ c. full of meanness.

2. Hepzibah's face was
   - ☐ a. wet with tears.
   - ☐ b. covered with scars.
   - ☐ c. hidden by a veil.

3. The guest approaching the room
   - ☐ a. banged on the stairs.
   - ☐ b. coughed nervously.
   - ☐ c. stopped several times.

4. Hepzibah desperately wanted Phoebe to be
   - ☐ a. grateful.
   - ☐ b. respectful.
   - ☐ c. cheerful.

5. Hepzibah's behavior made Phoebe
   - ☐ a. angry.
   - ☐ b. nervous.
   - ☐ c. tranquil.

Understanding the Passage

6. Apparently, Hepzibah had just
   - ☐ a. spoken harshly to Phoebe.
   - ☐ b. given Phoebe a gift.
   - ☐ c. spoken to Clifford.

7. Phoebe did not know for sure
   - ☐ a. who was in the passageway.
   - ☐ b. if Hepzibah was really her cousin.
   - ☐ c. what time of day it was.

8. As the guest approached the room, Hepzibah grew
   - ☐ a. tired of waiting.
   - ☐ b. extremely distressed.
   - ☐ c. increasingly angry.

9. Phoebe had apparently heard
   - ☐ a. music coming from the entryway.
   - ☐ b. footsteps in the night.
   - ☐ c. Hepzibah and Clifford fighting.

10. Hepzibah was concerned about the impression she would make on
   - ☐ a. Phoebe.
   - ☐ b. the approaching guest.
   - ☐ c. her children.

The animals had begun to climb up again toward the bushes, some skipping gaily over everything, others stopping to taste the tender herbs.

"Peter," Heidi said presently, "the prettiest of all are Little Swan and Little Bear."

"I know," Peter replied. "The uncle brushes and washes them, and gives them salt, and has the nicest shed."

Suddenly Peter jumped up and bounded after the goats. Heidi followed. Something must have happened and she simply could not stay behind. Peter forced his way through the middle of the herd to that side of the Alm where the bare and jagged rock fell away steeply. Here, a heedless little goat might easily tumble down and break his legs. Peter had noticed inquisitive little Goldfinch jumping in that direction. The boy arrived just in time, for the little goat was just about to jump toward the edge of the precipice. Peter, lunging toward the goat, fell down and only managed to seize one of its legs as he fell. Goldfinch gave an angry cry at finding herself caught up and tried desperately to free herself. Peter could not get up and shouted for Heidi to help because he was afraid Goldfinch might wrench her leg. Heidi was already there and at once saw the danger. She quickly gathered some sweet-smelling plants from the ground and held them out toward Goldfinch, saying coaxingly, "Come along, Goldfinch, and be good! Look! You might fall down and hurt yourself."

The little goat turned quickly and ate the herbs from Heidi's outstretched hand. In the meantime Peter got to his feet again and held Goldfinch by the cord with which her little bell was fastened to her neck. Heidi grasped the goat in the same way at the other side of its head and together they led the truant back to the peacefully grazing flock. As soon as Peter got her back to safety, he raised his stick and started to give her a good beating. Goldfinch, however, knowing what was in store, timidly shrank back, and Heidi cried, "No, Peter! No! You mustn't beat her! Look how frightened she is!"

"She deserves it," Peter muttered, about to strike; but Heidi threw herself against his arm, crying indignantly, "Don't touch her! You will hurt her! Leave her alone!"

Peter turned surprised eyes on the fierce little girl and his stick dropped to his side. "All right, then, I'll let her off."

Recalling Facts

1. Little Swan and Little Bear were
   - ☐ a. stubborn.
   - ☐ b. pretty.
   - ☐ c. fearless.

2. Goldfinch was
   - ☐ a. the prettiest of all.
   - ☐ b. timid.
   - ☐ c. inquisitive.

3. Peter managed to seize Goldfinch by its
   - ☐ a. leg.
   - ☐ b. tail.
   - ☐ c. ear.

4. Heidi helped rescue Goldfinch by offering the goat some
   - ☐ a. candy.
   - ☐ b. oats.
   - ☐ c. herbs.

5. Peter agreed not to
   - ☐ a. beat the goat.
   - ☐ b. be so cautious.
   - ☐ c. leave the herd unattended.

Understanding the Passage

6. The goats were apparently
   - ☐ a. grazing in the mountains.
   - ☐ b. returning to the farmyard.
   - ☐ c. jumping through a garden.

7. Peter saved Goldfinch from
   - ☐ a. a good beating.
   - ☐ b. hurting herself.
   - ☐ c. eating the harmful herbs.

8. After Peter grabbed Goldfinch, she tried to
   - ☐ a. break away.
   - ☐ b. nuzzle him.
   - ☐ c. jump off the edge.

9. Goldfinch was saved by
   - ☐ a. Peter.
   - ☐ b. Heidi.
   - ☐ c. both a and b.

10. Peter was used to
    - ☐ a. receiving instructions from Heidi.
    - ☐ b. disciplining goats.
    - ☐ c. both a and b.

from **Alice's Adventures in Wonderland** *by Lewis Carroll*

A large rose tree stood near the entrance of the garden. The roses growing on it were white, but there were three gardeners at it, busily painting them red. Alice thought this was a very curious thing, and she went nearer to watch them, and, just as she came up to them, she heard one of them say "Look out now, Five! Don't go splashing paint over me like that!"

"I couldn't help it," said Five, in a sulky tone. "Seven jogged my elbow."

On which Seven looked up and said, "That's right, Five! Always lay the blame on others!"

"*You'd* better not talk!" said Five. "I heard the Queen say only yesterday you deserved to be beheaded."

"What for?" said the one who had spoken first.

"That's none of *your* business, Two!" said Seven.

"Yes it *is* his business!" said Five. "And I'll tell him—it was for bringing the cook tulip roots instead of onions."

Seven flung down his brush, and had just begun "Well, of all the unjust things—" when his eye chanced to fall upon Alice, as she stood watching them, and he checked himself suddenly: the others looked round also, and all of them bowed low.

"Would you tell me, please," said Alice, a little timidly, "why you are painting those roses?"

Five and Seven said nothing, but looked at Two. Two began, in a low voice, "Why, the fact is, you see, Miss, this here ought to have been a *red* rose tree, and we put a white one in by mistake; and, if the Queen was to find it out, we should all have our heads cut off, you know. So you see, Miss, we're doing our best, afore she comes, to—" At this moment, Five, who had been anxiously looking across the garden, called out "The Queen! The Queen!" and the three gardeners instantly threw themselves flat upon their faces. There was a sound of many footsteps, and Alice looked round, eager to see the Queen.

First came ten soldiers carrying clubs: these were all shaped like the three gardeners, oblong and flat, with their hands and feet at the corners: next the ten courtiers: these were ornamented all over with diamonds, and walked two by two, as the soldiers did. After these came the royal children: there were ten of them, and the little dears came jumping merrily along, hand in hand, in couples.

Recalling Facts

1. The three gardeners were
   - ☐ a. putting red paint on white roses.
   - ☐ b. putting white paint on the garden gate.
   - ☐ c. planting new rose trees.

2. Seven gave the cook tulip roots instead of
   - ☐ a. rose petals.
   - ☐ b. onions.
   - ☐ c. a paintbrush.

3. When they saw the Queen coming, the three gardeners
   - ☐ a. ran away.
   - ☐ b. hid behind Alice.
   - ☐ c. threw themselves on the ground.

4. The ten soldiers carried
   - ☐ a. rose trees.
   - ☐ b. guns.
   - ☐ c. clubs.

5. The royal children were
   - ☐ a. ornamented with diamonds.
   - ☐ b. holding hands.
   - ☐ c. dressed in white.

Understanding the Passage

6. The three gardeners were
   - ☐ a. in love with the Queen.
   - ☐ b. sons of the Queen.
   - ☐ c. afraid of the Queen.

7. The soldiers and courtiers led the way for the
   - ☐ a. guests of the palace.
   - ☐ b. gardeners.
   - ☐ c. royal family.

8. The Queen was apparently not a
   - ☐ a. forgiving person.
   - ☐ b. powerful person.
   - ☐ c. demanding person.

9. The gardeners' bodies were
   - ☐ a. round.
   - ☐ b. rectangular.
   - ☐ c. square.

10. The gardeners hoped to paint the rose tree before
   - ☐ a. the end of the year.
   - ☐ b. Alice had to leave.
   - ☐ c. the Queen discovered their mistake.

Ramona was wan and haggard. She had scarcely slept. The idea had taken possession of her that Alessandro was dead. On the sixth and seventh days she had walked each afternoon far down the river road, by which he would be sure to come; down the meadows, and by the crosscut, out to the highway; at each step straining her tearful eyes into the distance—the cruel, blank, silent distance. She had come back after dark, whiter and more wan than she went out. As she sat at the supper table, silent, making no feint of eating, only drinking glass after glass of milk, in thirsty haste, even Margarita pitied her. But the Señora did not. She thought the best things which could happen, would be that the Indian should never come back. Ramona would recover from it in a little while; the mortification would be the worst thing, but even that, time would heal. She wondered that the girl had not more pride than to let her wretchedness be so plainly seen. She herself would have died before she would go about with such a woebegone face, for a whole household to see and gossip about.

On the morning of the eighth day, Ramona, desperate, stopped Felipe, as he was going down the veranda steps. The Señora was in the garden, and saw them; but Ramona did not care. "Felipe!" she cried. "I must, I must speak to you! Do you think Alessandro is dead? What else could keep him from coming?" Her lips were dry, her cheeks scarlet, her voice husky. A few more days of this, and she would be in a brain fever, Felipe thought, as he looked compassionately at her.

"Oh, no, no, dear! Do not think that!" he replied. "A thousand things might have kept him."

"Ten thousand things would not! Nothing could!" said Ramona. "I know he is dead. Can't you send a messenger, Felipe, and see?"

The Señora was walking toward them. She overheard the last words. Looking toward Felipe, no more regarding Ramona than if she had not been within sight or hearing, the Señora said, "It seems to me that would not be quite consistent with dignity. How does it strike you, Felipe? If you thought best, we might spare a man as soon as the vintage is over, I suppose."

Ramona walked away. The vintage would not be over for a week.

Recalling Facts

1. Ramona feared that Alessandro
   - ☐ a. no longer liked her.
   - ☐ b. had run away with Margarita.
   - ☐ c. was dead.

2. Each afternoon Ramona looked for Alessandro
   - ☐ a. out on the highway.
   - ☐ b. up in the mountains.
   - ☐ c. on every street in town.

3. The Señora hoped the Indian
   - ☐ a. would never come back.
   - ☐ b. would marry Ramona.
   - ☐ c. would apologize to Felipe.

4. Ramona asked Felipe to
   - ☐ a. make her something to eat.
   - ☐ b. help with the vintage.
   - ☐ c. send a messenger to look for Alessandro.

5. Felipe feared that Ramona would soon
   - ☐ a. disappear.
   - ☐ b. develop brain fever.
   - ☐ c. forget to do the milking.

Understanding the Passage

6. Alessandro was
   - ☐ a. the Señora's best friend.
   - ☐ b. an Indian.
   - ☐ c. owner of the ranch.

7. With Alessandro missing, Ramona
   - ☐ a. ate more than ever.
   - ☐ b. lost her appetite.
   - ☐ c. learned how to cook.

8. The Señora considered herself to be a
   - ☐ a. woman of pride.
   - ☐ b. kind woman.
   - ☐ c. forgiving woman.

9. Felipe tried to
   - ☐ a. hurt Ramona.
   - ☐ b. comfort Ramona.
   - ☐ c. amuse Ramona.

10. Ramona hoped a messenger could be sent out
    - ☐ a. when the vintage was over.
    - ☐ b. at the end of the week.
    - ☐ c. right away.

We entered the Indian Ocean and steered northerly for Java Head. The winds were light. Weeks slipped by. She crawled on, do or die, and people at home began to think of posting us overdue.

One Saturday evening, I being off duty, the men asked me to give them an extra bucket of water or so—for washing clothes. As I did not wish to screw on the freshwater pump so late, I went forward whistling, and with a key in my hand to unlock the forepeak scuttle, intending to serve the water out of a spare tank we kept there.

The smell down below was as unexpected as it was frightful. One would have thought hundreds of paraffin lamps had been flaring and smoking in that hole for days. I was glad to get out. The man with me coughed and said, "Funny smell, sir." I answered negligently, "It's good for the health, they say," and walked aft.

The first thing I did was to put my head down the square of the midship ventilator. As I lifted the lid a visible breath, something like a thin fog, a puff of faint haze, rose from the opening. The ascending air was hot, and had a heavy, sooty, paraffiny smell. I gave one sniff, and put down the lid gently. It was no use choking myself. The cargo was on fire.

Next day she began to smoke in earnest. You see it was to be expected, for though the coal was of a safe kind, that cargo had been so handled, so broken up with handling, that it looked more like smithy coal than anything else. Then it had been wetted—more than once. It rained all the time we were taking it back from the hulk, and now with this long passage it got heated, and it was a case of spontaneous combustion.

The captain called us into the cabin. He had a chart spread on the table, and looked unhappy. He said, "The coast of West Australia is near, but I mean to proceed to our destination. It is the hurricane month too, but we will just keep her head for Bangkok and fight the fire. We will try first to stifle this damned combustion by want of air."

We tried. We battened down everything and still she smoked. The smoke kept coming out through imperceptible crevices.

Recalling Facts

1. The speaker went to get water so the men could
   - ☐ a. take a bath.
   - ☐ b. ease their thirst.
   - ☐ c. wash their clothes.

2. The speaker was the one who
   - ☐ a. discovered the fire.
   - ☐ b. started the fire.
   - ☐ c. put out the fire.

3. The burning cargo smelled like
   - ☐ a. fish oil.
   - ☐ b. paraffin.
   - ☐ c. rubber.

4. The ship was traveling during the
   - ☐ a. hurricane month.
   - ☐ b. dry season.
   - ☐ c. coldest week of the year.

5. The captain decided to
   - ☐ a. keep sailing toward Bangkok.
   - ☐ b. turn toward West Australia.
   - ☐ c. abandon ship immediately.

Understanding the Passage

6. The speaker first suspected a problem when
   - ☐ a. the ship entered the Indian Ocean.
   - ☐ b. the captain called him.
   - ☐ c. he noticed a funny smell.

7. The smoke was coming from burning
   - ☐ a. wood.
   - ☐ b. coal.
   - ☐ c. oil.

8. The cargo caught fire in part because
   - ☐ a. it had gotten wet.
   - ☐ b. someone dropped a match on it.
   - ☐ c. the ship's ventilator was broken.

9. The fire was discovered during a
   - ☐ a. three-hour cruise.
   - ☐ b. midnight party.
   - ☐ c. long trip.

10. The crew tried to put the fire out by
   - ☐ a. smothering it.
   - ☐ b. throwing water on it.
   - ☐ c. pouring sand on it.

from **Under the Lilacs** *by Louisa May Alcott*

The small door of the coach house was fastened inside, but the large one had a padlock on it. Mrs. Moss quickly unfastened it, and the little girls ran in. They were playing on the long-coveted old carriage when suddenly they heard a noise.

"Who is there?" demanded Mrs. Moss, in a stern tone, backing toward the door with both children clinging to her skirts.

"Come out this minute, or I shall have to come and get you," she called again, growing very brave all of a sudden as she caught sight of a pair of small, dusty shoes under the coach.

"Yes, 'm, I'm coming as fast as I can," answered a meek voice, as what appeared to be a bundle of rags leaped out of the dark, followed by a poodle, who immediately sat down at the bare feet of his owner with a watchful air, as if ready to assault anyone who might approach too near.

"Now, then, who are you, and how did you get here?" asked Mrs. Moss, trying to speak sternly, though her motherly eyes were already full of pity as they rested on the forlorn little figure before her.

"Please, 'm, my name is Ben Brown, and I'm travelin'."

"Where are you going?"

"Anywheres to get work."

"What sort of work can you do?"

"All kinds. I'm used to horses."

"Bless me! Such a little chap as you?"

"I'm twelve, ma'am, and can ride anything on four legs"; and the small boy gave a nod that seemed to say, "Bring on your Cruisers. I'm ready for 'em."

"Haven't you got any folks?" asked Mrs. Moss, amused but still anxious, for the sunburnt face was very thin, the eyes hollow with hunger or pain, and the ragged figure leaned on the wheel as if too weak or weary to stand alone.

"No, 'm, not of my own; and the people I was left with beat me, so I run away." The last words seemed to bolt out against his will, as if the woman's sympathy irresistibly won the child's confidence.

"Then I don't blame you. But how did you get here?"

"I was so tired I couldn't go any further, and I thought the folks up here at the big house would take me in. But the gate was locked, and I was so discouraged, I jest laid down outside and give up."

Recalling Facts

1. The girls were playing in the
   - ☐ a. gatehouse.
   - ☐ b. coach house.
   - ☐ c. guesthouse.

2. The boy was accompanied by a
   - ☐ a. golden retriever.
   - ☐ b. poodle.
   - ☐ c. collie.

3. Ben Brown had no
   - ☐ a. parents.
   - ☐ b. experience with horses.
   - ☐ c. both a and b.

4. Ben was
   - ☐ a. 10 years old.
   - ☐ b. 12 years old.
   - ☐ c. 15 years old.

5. Ben had hoped the people at the big house would
   - ☐ a. take him in.
   - ☐ b. find his parents.
   - ☐ c. remember him.

Understanding the Passage

6. When the girls heard a noise, they became
   - ☐ a. excited.
   - ☐ b. friendly.
   - ☐ c. frightened.

7. Ben Brown had
   - ☐ a. once been rich.
   - ☐ b. lived a hard life.
   - ☐ c. friends in many places.

8. Ben was
   - ☐ a. disagreeable.
   - ☐ b. cooperative.
   - ☐ c. threatening.

9. After hearing Ben's story, Mrs. Moss felt
   - ☐ a. angry with Ben.
   - ☐ b. disappointed in Ben.
   - ☐ c. sorry for Ben.

10. Ben's dog appeared ready to
    - ☐ a. run away.
    - ☐ b. defend Ben.
    - ☐ c. make friends.

When the light was fading, and Mrs. Morel could see no more to sew, she rose and went to the door. Everywhere was the sound of excitement, the restlessness of the holiday, that at last infected her. She went out into the side garden. Women were coming home from the wakes, the children hugging a white lamb with green legs, or a wooden horse. Occasionally a man lurched past, almost as full as he could carry. Sometimes a good husband came along with his family, peacefully. But usually the women and children were alone. The stay-at-home mothers stood gossiping at the corners of the alley, as the twilight sank, folding their arms under their white aprons.

Mrs. Morel was alone, but she was used to it. Her son and her little girl slept upstairs; so, it seemed, her home was there behind her, fixed and stable. But she felt wretched with the coming child. The world seemed a dreary place, where nothing else would happen for her—at least until William grew up. But for herself, nothing but this dreary endurance—till the children grew up. And the children! She could not afford to have this third. She did not want it. The father was serving beer in a public house, swilling himself drunk. She despised him, and was tied to him. This coming child was too much for her. If it were not for William and Annie, she was sick of it, the struggle with poverty and ugliness and meanness.

She went into the front garden, feeling too heavy to take herself out, yet unable to stay indoors. The heat suffocated her. And looking ahead, the prospect of her life made her feel as if she were buried alive.

The front garden was a small square with a private hedge. There she stood, trying to soothe herself with the scent of flowers and the fading, beautiful evening. Opposite her small gate was the stile that led uphill, under the tall hedge between the burning glow of the cut pastures. The sky overhead throbbed and pulsed with light. The glow sank quickly off the field; the earth and the hedges smoked dusk. As it grew dark, a ruddy glare came out on the hilltop, and out of the glare the diminished commotion of the fair. Sometimes, down the trough of darkness formed by the path under the hedges, men came lurching home.

Recalling Facts

1. Most of the women and children in the streets
   - ☐ a. were accompanied by men.
   - ☐ b. seemed excited.
   - ☐ c. were coming to visit Mrs. Morel.

2. Mrs. Morel had
   - ☐ a. two girls.
   - ☐ b. a boy and a girl.
   - ☐ c. two boys.

3. Mrs. Morel was expecting
   - ☐ a. her husband.
   - ☐ b. guests for dinner.
   - ☐ c. another child.

4. Mrs. Morel was feeling
   - ☐ a. miserable.
   - ☐ b. satisfied.
   - ☐ c. challenged.

5. The events in the passage took place in the
   - ☐ a. early morning.
   - ☐ b. early evening.
   - ☐ c. afternoon.

Understanding the Passage

6. The narrator implies that a good husband
   - ☐ a. works hard.
   - ☐ b. spends time with his family.
   - ☐ c. tills the family garden.

7. Mrs. Morel saw
   - ☐ a. her husband serving beer.
   - ☐ b. her husband lurching down the road.
   - ☐ c. very little of her husband.

8. Mrs. Morel looked forward to the day when
   - ☐ a. her husband would get a regular job.
   - ☐ b. she would have another baby.
   - ☐ c. her children were grown up.

9. Mrs. Morel did not feel she could
   - ☐ a. talk openly to her doctor.
   - ☐ b. leave her husband.
   - ☐ c. love William and Annie.

10. The one thing that kept Mrs. Morel from complete despair was her love for her
    - ☐ a. children.
    - ☐ b. husband.
    - ☐ c. home.

from **The Land of Oz** *by L. Frank Baum*

Old Mombi returned home earlier than usual. She had met a crooked wizard who resided in a lonely cave in the mountains. She had traded several important secrets of magic with him. Having in this way secured three new recipes, four magical powders, and a selection of herbs of wonderful power and potency, she hobbled home as fast as she could.

So intent was Mombi on the treasures she had gained that when she turned the bend in the road and caught a glimpse of the man, she merely nodded and said: "Good evening, sir." But, after a moment, Mombi noticed that the person did not move or reply. She cast a shrewd glance into his face and discovered his pumpkin head—elaborately carved by Tip's jackknife. "Heh!" cried Mombi, giving a sort of grunt; "that rascally boy has been playing tricks again! Very good! ve—ry *good!* I'll beat him black and blue for trying to scare me in this fashion!"

Angrily she raised her stick to smash in the grinning pumpkin head of the dummy. But a sudden thought made her pause, the uplifted stick left motionless in the air.

"Why, here is a good chance to try my new powder!" said she, eagerly. "And then I can tell whether that crooked wizard has fairly traded secrets, or whether he has fooled me as wickedly as I fooled him."

After some search Mombi drew from her basket an old pepperbox, upon the faded label of which the wizard had written with a lead pencil: "Powder of Life." "Ah—here it is!" she cried, joyfully. "And now let us see if it is potent. The stingy wizard didn't give me much of it. But I guess there's enough for two or three doses."

Then Mombi lifted her left hand, with its little finger pointed upward, and said: "Weaugh!" Then she lifted her right hand, with the thumb pointed upward, and said: "Teaugh!" Then she lifted both hands, with all the fingers and thumbs spread out, and cried: "Peaugh!"

Jack Pumpkinhead stepped back a pace, at this, and said in a reproachful voice: "Don't yell like that! Do you think I'm deaf?"

Old Mombi danced around him, frantic with delight. "He lives!" she screamed: "he lives! he lives!" Then she threw her stick into the air and caught it as it came down; and she hugged herself with both arms.

Recalling Facts

1. Mombi made a trade with
   - ☐ a. a wizard.
   - ☐ b. Tip.
   - ☐ c. Jack Pumpkinhead.

2. The man Mombi saw in the road was really
   - ☐ a. Tip.
   - ☐ b. a pumpkin head.
   - ☐ c. the crooked wizard.

3. The pumpkin head had been carved by
   - ☐ a. Mombi.
   - ☐ b. Jack.
   - ☐ c. Tip.

4. Mombi wanted to use the pumpkin head to try out her new
   - ☐ a. herbs.
   - ☐ b. powder.
   - ☐ c. broom.

5. Jack told Mombi not to
   - ☐ a. raise her stick.
   - ☐ b. sprinkle powder.
   - ☐ c. yell so loudly.

Understanding the Passage

6. Mombi appears to be some kind of
   - ☐ a. animal lover.
   - ☐ b. witch.
   - ☐ c. doctor.

7. Mombi was determined to get even with
   - ☐ a. Jack Pumpkinhead.
   - ☐ b. the witch doctor.
   - ☐ c. Tip.

8. Apparently, Mombi
   - ☐ a. had a kind and gentle soul.
   - ☐ b. was distrustful of others.
   - ☐ c. had been tricked by the wizard.

9. "Weaugh," "Teaugh," and "Peaugh" were
   - ☐ a. the names of the herbs.
   - ☐ b. varieties of pumpkins.
   - ☐ c. magic words.

10. Mombi
   - ☐ a. brought Jack to life.
   - ☐ b. was very angry with the wizard.
   - ☐ c. screamed in horror when Jack spoke.

It got lonesomer and lonesomer. There was the big sky up there, empty and awful deep; and the ocean down there without a thing on it but just the waves. All around us was a ring, where the sky and the water come together; yes, a monstrous big ring it was, and we right in the dead center of it—plumb in the center. We was racing along like a prairie fire. But it never made any difference, we couldn't seem to git past that center no way. I couldn't see that we ever gained an inch on that ring. It made a body feel creepy. It was so curious and unaccountable.

Well, everything was so awful still that we got to talking in a very low voice, and kept on getting creepier and lonesomer and less and less talky, till at last the talk ran dry altogether, and we just set there and "thunk," as Jim calls it, and never said a word for the longest time.

The professor never stirred till the sun was overhead; then he stood up and put a kind of triangle to his eye, and Tom said it was a sextant and he was taking the sun to see whereabouts the balloon was. Then he ciphered a little and looked in a book, and then he begun to carry on again. He said lots of wild things, and, among others, he said he would keep up this hundred-mile gait till the middle of tomorrow afternoon, and then he'd land in London.

We said we would be humbly thankful.

He was turning away, but he whirled around when we said that, and give us a long look of his blackest kind—one of the maliciousest and suspiciousest looks I ever see. Then he says:

"You want to leave me. Don't try to deny it."

We didn't know what to say, so we held in and didn't say nothing at all.

He went aft and set down, but he couldn't seem to git that thing out of his mind. Every now and then he would rip out something about it, and try to make us answer him, but we dasn't.

It got lonesomer and lonesomer right along, and it did seem to me I couldn't stand it. It was still worse when night begun to come on. By and by Tom pinched me and whispers:

"Look!"

Recalling Facts

1. The balloon was sailing over
   - ☐ a. the mountains.
   - ☐ b. a large desert.
   - ☐ c. an ocean.

2. The balloonists felt they were in the center of a
   - ☐ a. big ring.
   - ☐ b. huge storm.
   - ☐ c. deep fog.

3. The professor finally stirred when the sun
   - ☐ a. had risen.
   - ☐ b. was setting.
   - ☐ c. was overhead.

4. The professor said he expected to land in London
   - ☐ a. later that day.
   - ☐ b. the following afternoon.
   - ☐ c. next Friday.

5. Just as night was coming on, Tom
   - ☐ a. fell asleep.
   - ☐ b. spoke to the professor.
   - ☐ c. whispered to the narrator.

Understanding the Passage

6. According to the professor, the balloon was
   - ☐ a. hardly moving.
   - ☐ b. going slowly.
   - ☐ c. moving very fast.

7. The narrator felt that the balloon was
   - ☐ a. going too fast.
   - ☐ b. making no real progress.
   - ☐ c. flying too high.

8. Tom and the narrator were
   - ☐ a. confident.
   - ☐ b. nervous.
   - ☐ c. fearful.

9. The professor seemed to be
   - ☐ a. angry with the boys.
   - ☐ b. totally lost.
   - ☐ c. both a and b.

10. The professor could not get the boys to
    - ☐ a. use the sextant.
    - ☐ b. confess their true feelings.
    - ☐ c. stop talking.

from **The Vanishing American** *by Zane Grey*

It was hunger that reminded Marian of the passing hours and discovered to her that she had ridden until noon. Five hours of steady riding! At four miles an hour she had in all covered twenty miles. She wondered if Buckskin was tired. He paced on, steadfast and leisurely. Marian had her sandwich and bit of chocolate, and a drink from her canteen. It was the need of anything that made it precious. When before in her life had a dusty, black-crusted biscuit seemed at once a pleasure and a blessing? How often had she no taste for chocolate! And as for water and its wonderful, refreshing power, she had known nothing. There must be a time then for food, for drink to mean a great deal. And if for these, why not for all things?

As Marian rode on, pondering thoughts thus evolved, all at once she looked up to see a tremendous gash in the green-forested earth ahead. Withers, on foot, was waiting for her on the brink of a chasm. Far across Marian saw the opposite rim, a red-gold, barefaced cliff, sheering downward. She was amazed. The very earth seemed to have opened. As she rode up to Withers the chasm deepened to astonishing depths and still she could not see the bottom. The trader halted her before she got to the rim.

"Pahute Canyon," he said. "And it's bad medicine. You've got to walk fast. Because the horses can't go slow and I'll have to head them. Be sure to keep me in sight. Otherwise you might lose the trail."

Marian dismounted and handing her bridle to the trader she walked to the rim. A ghastly and naked glaring canyon yawned beneath her, tremendously wide and deep, bare of vegetation and blazing with its denuded and colored slopes.

"White people don't get to see Pahute Canyon," said Withers, as he gazed from beside her. "It's the wildest and most beautiful in the West. Reckon it'll be shore a spell before automobile tourists will drive in and out of here, eh?"

He laughed grimly, with some note of gratification in his voice. Marian felt speech difficult. She was astounded. Pictures of grand canyons could not convey any adequate conception of what was given by actual sight.

"Wonderful! Fearful!" exclaimed Marian, feeling the strange drawing power of the depths. "Oh, it seems impossible even to—to *slide* down there."

Recalling Facts

1. Marian had covered
   □ a. five miles.
   □ b. ten miles.
   □ c. twenty miles.

2. The name of Marian's horse was
   □ a. Canyon.
   □ b. Buckskin.
   □ c. Steadfast.

3. Marian ate some
   □ a. bananas.
   □ b. chocolate.
   □ c. nuts.

4. Withers was
   □ a. following Marian.
   □ b. standing on the rim of the chasm.
   □ c. hidden from view.

5. Withers was
   □ a. a trader.
   □ b. an official guide to Pahute Canyon.
   □ c. a fellow traveler.

Understanding the Passage

6. Apparently, Marian had never
   □ a. ridden a horse before.
   □ b. gone hungry before.
   □ c. been willing to travel before.

7. The chasm was
   □ a. an unexpected obstacle.
   □ b. very steep and very broad.
   □ c. the only one in the area.

8. Withers thought that Pahute Canyon was
   □ a. a dangerous place.
   □ b. a good place to camp.
   □ c. spoiled by tourists.

9. In terms of traveling through the area, Withers was
   □ a. more experienced than Marian.
   □ b. as inexperienced as Marian.
   □ c. less experienced than Marian.

10. The sight of Pahute Canyon
    □ a. bored Marian.
    □ b. depressed Marian.
    □ c. fascinated Marian.

from **The Posthumous Papers of the Pickwick Club** *by Charles Dickens*

"By-the-bye, Bob," said Hopkins, "we had a curious accident last night. A child was brought in, who had swallowed a necklace."

"Swallowed what, sir?" interrupted Mr. Pickwick.

"A necklace," replied Hopkins. "Not all at once, you know, that would be too much—*you* couldn't swallow that! No, the way was this. Child's parents were poor people who lived in a court. Child's eldest sister bought a necklace; common necklace, made of large black wooden beads. Child, being fond of toys, cribbed the necklace, hid it, played with it, cut the string, and swallowed a bead. Child thought it capital fun, went back next day, and swallowed another bead."

"Bless my heart," said Mr. Pickwick, "what a dreadful thing! I beg your pardon, sir. Go on."

"Next day, child swallowed two beads; the day after that, he treated himself to three, and so on, till in a week's time he had got through the necklace—five-and-twenty beads in all. The sister, who was an industrious girl, and seldom treated herself to a bit of finery, cried her eyes out at the loss of the necklace; looked high and low for it; but, I needn't say, didn't find it. A few days afterwards, the family was at dinner—baked shoulder of mutton, and potatoes under it. The child, who wasn't hungry, was playing about the room, when suddenly there was heard a devil of a noise, like a small hailstorm. 'Don't do that, my boy,' said the father. 'I ain't a-doin' nothing,' said the child. 'Well, don't do it again,' said the father. There was a short silence, and then the noise began again, worse than ever. 'If you don't mind what I say, my boy,' said the father, 'you'll find yourself in bed, in something less than a pig's whisper.' He gave the child a shake to make him obedient, and such a rattling ensued as nobody ever heard before. 'Why, it's *in* the child!' said the father; 'he's got the croup in the wrong place!' 'No I haven't, father,' said the child, beginning to cry, 'it's the necklace; I swallowed it, father.' The father caught the child up, and ran with him to the hospital: the beads in the boy's stomach rattling all the way with the jolting; and the people looking up in the air, and down in the cellars, to see where the unusual sound was coming from."

Recalling Facts

1. The beads on the necklace
   were made from
   ☐ a. stones.
   ☐ b. wood.
   ☐ c. shells.

2. The color of the beads was
   ☐ a. green.
   ☐ b. brown.
   ☐ c. black.

3. On the first day, the child
   swallowed
   ☐ a. one bead.
   ☐ b. two beads.
   ☐ c. three beads.

4. In all, the child swallowed
   ☐ a. fifteen beads.
   ☐ b. twenty beads.
   ☐ c. twenty-five beads.

5. The child was rushed to the
   hospital by his
   ☐ a. father.
   ☐ b. mother.
   ☐ c. sister.

Understanding the Passage

6. The child enjoyed
   ☐ a. hurting his sister.
   ☐ b. a wholesome dinner.
   ☐ c. swallowing beads.

7. The child's sister
   ☐ a. had few possessions.
   ☐ b. did not like her brother.
   ☐ c. never wore the
        necklace.

8. The child wasn't hungry
   because
   ☐ a. his stomach was full
        of beads.
   ☐ b. he had just eaten some
        potatoes.
   ☐ c. the smell of mutton
        made him sick.

9. At first, the father thought
   the child was
   ☐ a. sick.
   ☐ b. misbehaving.
   ☐ c. banging his drum.

10. The father knew something
    was very wrong when he
    ☐ a. sat down to dinner.
    ☐ b. entered the child's
         room.
    ☐ c. shook the child.

Ormond wished desperately to win the heart of Miss Florence Annaly. Was that heart free? He resolved to inquire first from his dear friend, Dr. Cambray, who was a great favorite with Florence, and so dearer than ever to Ormond. He went straight to see and consult him, and Ormond thought he was confiding a deep secret to the doctor, when first he spoke to him of his passion for Miss Annaly. To his surprise, however, the doctor told him he had seen it long ago. His wife and daughters had all discovered it, too, even when they were first with him at Annaly.

"Is it possible? And what do you all think?"

"We think that you would be a perfectly happy man, if you could win Miss Annaly; and we truly wish you success. But—"

"But—O my dear doctor, you alarm me beyond measure."

"What! By wishing you success?"

"No, but by something in your look and manner, and by that terrible but. You think that I shall never succeed—you think that her heart is engaged. If that be the case, tell me so at once, and I will set off for France tomorrow."

"My good sir, you are in too great a hurry to come to a conclusion before you have the means to do so."

"I will be patient all my life, if you will only this instant tell me whether she is engaged."

"I do not know whether Miss Annaly's heart be disengaged or not. I can tell you only that she has had a number of brilliant offers, and that she has refused them all."

"That proves that she had not found one amongst them that she liked," said Ormond.

"Or that she liked someone better than all those whom she refused," said Dr. Cambray.

"That is true—that is possible—that is a dreadful thought," said Ormond. "But do you think there is any truth in that?"

"There is, I am sorry to tell you, my dear Ormond, much going against you. I can form no opinion for I have had no opportunity of judging—I have never seen the two young people together. But there is a gentleman of great merit, of suitable family and fortune, who is deeply in love with Miss Annaly. I presume he has not been refused, for I understand he is soon to be here."

Recalling Facts

1. Dr. Cambray was
   - ☐ a. a close friend of Florence Annaly.
   - ☐ b. Ormond's personal physician.
   - ☐ c. Florence Annaly's father.

2. Dr. Cambray wished Ormond
   - ☐ a. success.
   - ☐ b. a long life.
   - ☐ c. prosperity.

3. Miss Annaly had received
   - ☐ a. invitations to many balls.
   - ☐ b. a large inheritance.
   - ☐ c. many offers of marriage.

4. Dr. Cambray did not know if Miss Annaly's heart was
   - ☐ a. engaged.
   - ☐ b. healthy.
   - ☐ c. broken.

5. The gentleman who was about to arrive came from
   - ☐ a. a suitable family.
   - ☐ b. average means.
   - ☐ c. humble beginnings.

Understanding the Passage

6. Ormond was surprised that Dr. Cambray
   - ☐ a. would speak so openly to him.
   - ☐ b. was not in favor of the match.
   - ☐ c. knew of his feelings for Miss Annaly.

7. Ormond was
   - ☐ a. impatient.
   - ☐ b. methodical.
   - ☐ c. uncontrollable.

8. Ormond hoped Dr. Cambray could give him
   - ☐ a. assistance in his business.
   - ☐ b. money for his trip to Florence.
   - ☐ c. an indication of Florence's feelings.

9. Dr. Cambray believed that Florence might be
   - ☐ a. in love with someone other than Ormond.
   - ☐ b. not ready for a serious engagement.
   - ☐ c. hiding her true feelings from her family.

10. Ormond planned to leave the country if
    - ☐ a. he could not improve on his career.
    - ☐ b. Miss Annaly had no interest in him.
    - ☐ c. Dr. Cambray requested him to do so.

The silence was broken by the clash of the garden gate, a tap at the door, and its opening. Christian Cantle appeared in the room in his Sunday clothes. He had been saying to them while the door was leaving its latch, "To think that I who go from home but once in a while, and hardly then, should have been there this morning."

"'Tis news you have brought us, then, Christian?" said Mrs. Yeobright.

"Ay, sure, about a witch, and ye must overlook my time o' day; for, says I, 'I must go and tell 'em, though they won't have had done dinner.' I assure ye it made me shake like a driven leaf. Do ye think any harm will come o' it?"

"Well—what?"

"This morning at church we was all standing up, and the parson said, 'Let us pray.' 'Well,' think I, 'one may as well kneel as stand;' so down I went; and, more than that, all the rest were as willing to oblige the man as I. We hadn't been hard at it for more than a minute when a most terrible screech sounded through church, as if somebody had given up their heart's blood. All the folk jumped up, and then we found that Susan Nunsuch had pricked Miss Vye with a long stocking needle, as she had threatened to do as soon as ever she could get the young lady to church, where she don't come very often. She've waited for this chance for weeks, so as to draw her blood and put an end to the bewitching of Susan's children that has been carried on so long. Sue followed her into church, sat next to her, and as soon as she could find a chance in went the stocking needle into my lady's arm."

"Good heaven, how horrid!" said Mrs. Yeobright.

"Sue pricked her that deep that the maid fainted away; and as I was afeared there might be some tumult among us, I got behind the bass viol and didn't see no more. But they carried her out into the air, 'tis said; but when they looked round for Sue she was gone. What a scream that girl gave, poor thing! There were the parson in his surplice holding up his hand and saying, 'Sit down, my good people, sit down!' But the deuce a bit would they sit down."

Recalling Facts

1. Christian brought news about
   - ☐ a. a witch.
   - ☐ b. a dinner invitation.
   - ☐ c. an accident.

2. While the people were praying,
   - ☐ a. it began to rain.
   - ☐ b. a terrible screech rang out.
   - ☐ c. the parson sang.

3. Susan Nunsuch stuck Miss Vye with a
   - ☐ a. knife.
   - ☐ b. hat pin.
   - ☐ c. stocking needle.

4. Miss Vye was stuck in the
   - ☐ a. neck.
   - ☐ b. leg.
   - ☐ c. arm.

5. The parson told the people to
   - ☐ a. leave the church.
   - ☐ b. pray for Miss Vye.
   - ☐ c. sit down.

Understanding the Passage

6. Christian apparently attended church
   - ☐ a. twice a week.
   - ☐ b. once a week.
   - ☐ c. rarely.

7. Mrs. Yeobright
   - ☐ a. did not attend church that Sunday.
   - ☐ b. was anxious to hear Christian's news.
   - ☐ c. both a and b.

8. Susan Nunsuch
   - ☐ a. wanted to stick Miss Vye in church.
   - ☐ b. wanted to kill Miss Vye.
   - ☐ c. didn't want to disturb the people at prayer.

9. Susan Nunsuch's action appeared to be
   - ☐ a. done on the spur of the moment.
   - ☐ b. well planned.
   - ☐ c. done on the orders of the parson.

10. The parson tried to
    - ☐ a. calm the people down.
    - ☐ b. clean Miss Vye's wound.
    - ☐ c. help Susan Nunsuch.

There was a great war, and the King had many soldiers but gave them small pay, so small that they could not live upon it, so three of them agreed among themselves to desert. One of them said to the others, "If we are caught we shall be hanged on the gallows. How shall we manage it?" Another said, "Look at that great cornfield; if we were to hide ourselves there, no one could find us. The troops are not allowed to enter it and tomorrow they are to march away." They crept into the corn; only the troops did not march away but remained lying all round about it. They stayed in the corn for two days and two nights, and were so hungry that they all but died, but if they had come out, their death would have been certain. Then said the soldiers, "What is the use of our deserting if we have to perish miserably here?" But now a fiery dragon came flying through the air. It came down to them and asked why they had concealed themselves there? They answered, "We are three soldiers who have deserted because the pay is so bad. Now we shall have to die of hunger if we stay here, or to dangle on the gallows if we go out." "If you will serve me for seven years," said the dragon, "I will convey you through the army so that no one shall seize you." "We have no choice and are compelled to accept," they replied. Then the dragon caught hold of them with his claws, carried them away through the air over the army and put them down again on the earth far from it. But the dragon was no other than the Devil. He gave them a small whip and said, "Whip with it and crack it, and then as much gold will spring up round about as you can wish for. Then you can live like great lords, keep horses, and drive your carriages, but when the seven years have come to an end, you are my property." Then he put before them a book which they were all three forced to sign. "I will, however, then set you a riddle," said he, "and if you can guess that, you shall be free and released from my power." Then the dragon flew away from them.

Recalling Facts

1. Three of the King's soldiers agreed to
   - ☐ a. fight.
   - ☐ b. die.
   - ☐ c. desert.

2. The three soldiers hid in a
   - ☐ a. cornfield.
   - ☐ b. barn.
   - ☐ c. forest.

3. The soldiers stayed hidden for
   - ☐ a. two days and nights.
   - ☐ b. three days and nights.
   - ☐ c. four days and nights.

4. The dragon asked the three soldiers to serve him for
   - ☐ a. three years.
   - ☐ b. five years.
   - ☐ c. seven years.

5. The dragon was really the
   - ☐ a. King.
   - ☐ b. Devil.
   - ☐ c. Lord of Horses.

Understanding the Passage

6. The soldiers felt that they should be
   - ☐ a. paid more.
   - ☐ b. fed better.
   - ☐ c. promoted.

7. Deserters from the army were
   - ☐ a. usually forgiven.
   - ☐ b. reduced in rank.
   - ☐ c. executed.

8. When the dragon found the soldiers, they were
   - ☐ a. happy.
   - ☐ b. discouraged.
   - ☐ c. desperate.

9. The soldiers
   - ☐ a. accepted the dragon's offer.
   - ☐ b. debated the dragon's offer.
   - ☐ c. rejected the dragon's offer.

10. If the soldiers couldn't solve the riddle, the dragon would
    - ☐ a. kill them.
    - ☐ b. possess them.
    - ☐ c. return them.

"I am not in the least sorry," said Evan, "I am very pleased."

"I really believe you are insane," said Mr. Vane, the police magistrate, indignantly. "What conceivable right have you to break other people's windows because their opinions don't agree with yours? Mr. Turnbull only gave expression to his sincere belief."

"So did I," said Evan MacIan.

"And who are you?" exploded Vane. "Are your views necessarily the right ones? Are you necessarily in possession of the truth?"

"Yes," said MacIan.

The magistrate broke into a contemptuous laugh.

"Oh, you want a nurse to look after you," he said. "You must pay £10."

Evan MacIan plunged his hands into his loose grey garments and drew out a queer-looking leather purse. It contained exactly twelve sovereigns. He paid down the ten, coin by coin, in silence, and equally silently returned the remaining two to the receptacle. Then he said, "May I say a word, your worship?"

Cumberland Vane seemed half hypnotized with the silence and automatic movements of the stranger; he made a movement with his head, which might have been either "yes" or "no." "I only wished to say, your worship," said MacIan, putting back the purse in his trouser pocket, "that smashing that shop window was, I confess, a useless and rather irregular business. It may be excused, however, as a mere preliminary to further proceedings, a sort of preface. Wherever and whenever I meet that man," and pointed to the editor of "The Atheist," "whether it be outside this door in ten minutes from now, or twenty years hence in some distant country, wherever and whenever I meet that man, I will fight him. Do not be afraid, I will not rush at him like a bully, or bear him down with any brute superiority. I will fight him like a gentleman; I will fight him as our fathers fought. He shall choose how, sword or pistol, horse or foot. But if he refuses, I will write his cowardice on every wall in the world. If he had said of my mother what he said of the Mother of God, there is not a club of clean men in Europe that would deny my right to call him out. If he had said it of my wife, you English would yourselves have pardoned me for beating him like a dog in the marketplace."

Recalling Facts

1. The magistrate thought that Evan was
   - ☐ a. guilty.
   - ☐ b. insane.
   - ☐ c. both a and b.

2. Evan's crime was
   - ☐ a. hitting Mr. Turnbull.
   - ☐ b. breaking a shop window.
   - ☐ c. swearing at the magistrate.

3. Evan's punishment was
   - ☐ a. a fine.
   - ☐ b. a prison sentence.
   - ☐ c. both a and b.

4. The editor of "The Atheist" was
   - ☐ a. Mr. Turnbull.
   - ☐ b. Mr. Vane.
   - ☐ c. Mr. MacIan.

5. Evan wanted only to fight
   - ☐ a. with swords.
   - ☐ b. on foot.
   - ☐ c. like a gentleman.

Understanding the Passage

6. Evan's crime showed that he was a
   - ☐ a. classic criminal.
   - ☐ b. mindless ruffian.
   - ☐ c. man with principles.

7. Evan's actions and comments
   - ☐ a. shocked the magistrate.
   - ☐ b. amused the magistrate.
   - ☐ c. angered the magistrate.

8. Evan accepted his punishment
   - ☐ a. angrily.
   - ☐ b. calmly.
   - ☐ c. smugly.

9. Evan said that his crime was
   - ☐ a. only a taste of things to come.
   - ☐ b. the act of a madman.
   - ☐ c. his first illegal act.

10. Evan and Mr. Turnbull had different opinions on
    - ☐ a. marriage.
    - ☐ b. politics.
    - ☐ c. religion.

This play was good, Harry. It was *Romeo and Juliet*. I must admit I was rather annoyed at the idea of seeing one of Shakespeare's plays done in such a wretched hole of a place. Still, I felt interested, in a sort of way. At any rate, I was determined to wait for the first act. There was a dreadful orchestra, presided over by a thin young man who sat at a cracked piano, that nearly drove me away, but at last the play began. Romeo was a stout elderly gentleman, with corked eyebrows and a figure like a beer barrel. ●
Mercutio was almost as bad. He was played by the low comedian, who had introduced gags of his own. They were both as grotesque as the scenery, and that looked as if it had come out of a country booth. But Juliet! Harry, imagine a girl, hardly seventeen years of age, with a little flowerlike face, a small Greek head with plaited coils of dark brown hair, eyes that were violet wells of passion, lips that were like the petals of a rose. She was the loveliest thing I had ever seen in my life. You said to me once that ●
pathos left you unmoved, but that beauty, mere beauty, could fill your eyes with tears. I tell you, Harry, I could hardly see this girl for the mist of tears that came across me. And her voice—I never heard such a voice. It was very low at first, with deep mellow notes, that seemed to fall singly upon one's ear. Then it became a little louder, and sounded like a flute. In the garden scene it had all the tremulous ecstasy that one hears just before dawn when nightingales are singing. There were moments, later on, when ●
it had the wild passion of violins. You know how a voice can stir one. The voice of Sibyl Vane is one thing that I shall never forget. Why should I not love her? Harry, I do love her. She is everything to me in life. Night after night I go to see her play. One evening she is Rosalind, and the next evening she is Imogen. Ordinary women never appeal to one's imagination. They are limited to their century. No glamour ever transfigures them. But an actress! How different an actress is! Harry! Why didn't you tell me that the only thing worth loving is an actress?

Recalling Facts

1. The man who played Romeo was a
   - ☐ a. stout elderly gentleman.
   - ☐ b. thin young lad.
   - ☐ c. pale middle-aged man.

2. Juliet was played by a
   - ☐ a. seventeen-year-old girl.
   - ☐ b. twenty-two-year-old woman.
   - ☐ c. thirty-year-old lady.

3. The speaker's tears were caused by
   - ☐ a. the theater's elegance.
   - ☐ b. Sibyl Vane's beauty.
   - ☐ c. the sad news Harry gave him.

4. The woman who played Juliet also played
   - ☐ a. Hebrews and Greeks.
   - ☐ b. Mercutio and Sibyl Vane.
   - ☐ c. Rosalind and Imogen.

5. The speaker decided that the only women worth loving were
   - ☐ a. rich women.
   - ☐ b. friends.
   - ☐ c. actresses.

Understanding the Passage

6. At first, the speaker did not think he would
   - ☐ a. understand *Romeo and Juliet.*
   - ☐ b. enjoy this version of *Romeo and Juliet.*
   - ☐ c. get a ticket to see *Romeo and Juliet.*

7. The actors who played Romeo and Mercutio
   - ☐ a. were world-famous performers.
   - ☐ b. never showed up for the performance.
   - ☐ c. were not very convincing.

8. The speaker thought Sibyl Vane's voice was
   - ☐ a. irritating.
   - ☐ b. too soft.
   - ☐ c. beautiful.

9. After seeing *Romeo and Juliet,* the speaker
   - ☐ a. returned to Paris.
   - ☐ b. went to see Sibyl Vane play other roles.
   - ☐ c. decided Harry was wrong about love.

10. The speaker thought actresses were
    - ☐ a. glamorous and exciting.
    - ☐ b. difficult to talk to.
    - ☐ c. impossible to love.

There was a man named Charley Roberts who traveled out of New York for an instantaneous water heater concern. For years he had been trying to sell old Townsend, but old Townsend said the heater ate up too much gas and would make the customers squawk. They squawked enough as it was. Roberts was a determined young man and kept after Townsend in spite of the latter's discouraging attitude.

Roberts was also a wisecracking, kidding New Yorker, who, when at home, lunched where his heroes lunched, just to be near them, look at them and overhear some of their wisecracks which he could repeat to his fellow drummers on the road. These heroes of his were comic strip artists, playwrights, and editors of humorous columns in the metropolitan press. His favorite column was the one conducted by George Balch in the *Standard* and when he was in the small towns, he frequently clipped silly items from the local papers and sent them to George. Charley had a tip that Old Man Townsend would be in Maysville on a certain day, so he took an interurban car thither and called at the gas office. Stephen Gale had just got back from a fruitless tour among the deadheads and was in the shop, behind the office, telling Ed Hunter that Mrs. Harper's pilot light wouldn't stay lighted.

Roberts, alone in the office, looked idly at Stephen's desk and saw a book. It was a volume of poems by Amy Lowell. A moment later Stephen reentered from the shop.

"Hello there, Gale," said Roberts.

"How are you, Mr. Roberts?" said Stephen.

"I heard the Old Man was here," said Roberts.

"You've missed him," said Stephen. "He was here yesterday afternoon and left for Haines City last night."

"Will he be here tomorrow?"

"I couldn't tell you. He's hard to keep track of."

"He's hard to sell, too. But I'll run over there and take a chance. I notice you've been reading highbrow poetry."

"I got this from the library."

"How do you like it?"

"I'm not strong for poetry that don't rhyme," said Stephen.

"I guess it's easier to write," said Roberts.

"I don't believe so. It isn't much trouble rhyming if you've got it in you. Look at Edgar Guest."

"How do you know he doesn't have trouble?"

"His works don't read like it," said Stephen. "Besides, I've tried it myself."

Recalling Facts

1. Roberts tried to sell Old Man Townsend a
   - ☐ a. gas pump.
   - ☐ b. neon sign.
   - ☐ c. water heater.

2. George Balch wrote
   - ☐ a. plays.
   - ☐ b. a newspaper column.
   - ☐ c. poems.

3. Roberts found a volume of poems by Amy Lowell
   - ☐ a. on Old Man Townsend's table.
   - ☐ b. on Stephen Gale's desk.
   - ☐ c. at the Maysville bookstore.

4. Old Man Townsend had left for
   - ☐ a. New York City.
   - ☐ b. Hunter City.
   - ☐ c. Haines City.

5. Roberts thought Lowell's poems were
   - ☐ a. familiar.
   - ☐ b. highbrow.
   - ☐ c. funny.

Understanding the Passage

6. Old Man Townsend
   - ☐ a. worked for the Haines City newspaper.
   - ☐ b. traveled frequently.
   - ☐ c. was loved by his customers.

7. Roberts liked to spend his time with
   - ☐ a. executives.
   - ☐ b. writers.
   - ☐ c. show girls.

8. The *Standard* seems to be a
   - ☐ a. poetry reading group.
   - ☐ b. major gas company.
   - ☐ c. newspaper.

9. Old Man Townsend
   - ☐ a. believed he needed a new water heater.
   - ☐ b. probably wanted to avoid Roberts.
   - ☐ c. was well loved by the people of Maysville.

10. Apparently, Stephen
    - ☐ a. worked for Old Man Townsend.
    - ☐ b. had read the poems Robert wrote.
    - ☐ c. had just bought a new water heater.

Nicholas's aunt had grown suspicious at his long disappearance, and had leapt to the conclusion that he had climbed over the wall behind the sheltering screen of the lilac bushes. She was now engaged in a rather hopeless search for him among the artichokes and raspberry canes.

"Nicholas, Nicholas!" she screamed, "you come out of this at once. It's no use trying to hide here. I can see you all the time."

It was probably the first time in twenty years that anyone had smiled in the lumber-room.

The angry repetitions of Nicholas's name gave way to a shriek, and a cry for somebody to come quickly. Nicholas shut the book, restored it carefully to its place in a corner, and shook some dust from a neighboring pile of newspapers over it. Then he crept from the lumber-room, locked the door, and replaced the key exactly where he had found it. His aunt was still calling his name when he sauntered into the front garden.

"Who's calling?" he asked.

"Me," came the answer from the other side of the wall; "didn't you hear me? I've been looking for you in the gooseberry garden, and I've slipped into the rainwater tank. Luckily there's no water in it, but the sides are slippery and I can't get out. Fetch the little ladder from under the cherry tree."

"I was told not to go into the gooseberry garden," said Nicholas.

"I told you not to, and now I tell you that you may," came the voice from the rainwater tank.

"Your voice doesn't sound like aunt's," objected Nicholas. "You may be the Evil One tempting me to be disobedient. Aunt often tells me that the Evil One tempts me and that I always yield. This time I'm not going to yield."

"Don't talk nonsense," said the prisoner in the tank. "Go and fetch the ladder."

"Will there be strawberry jam for tea?" asked Nicholas.

"Certainly there will be," said the aunt, privately resolving that Nicholas should have none of it.

"Now I know that you are the Evil One and not Aunt," shouted Nicholas gleefully. "When we asked Aunt for strawberry jam yesterday she said there wasn't any. I know there are four jars of it in the store cupboard, because I looked, and of course you know it's there, but *she* doesn't, because she said there wasn't any."

Recalling Facts

1. Nicholas's aunt looked for him in the
   - ☐ a. house.
   - ☐ b. barn.
   - ☐ c. garden.

2. When Nicholas heard his aunt's cry, he
   - ☐ a. continued reading.
   - ☐ b. shut his book.
   - ☐ c. ran to her rescue.

3. The aunt had slipped into a
   - ☐ a. muddy hole.
   - ☐ b. rainwater tank.
   - ☐ c. stone well.

4. Nicholas said that the voice sounded like the
   - ☐ a. Evil One.
   - ☐ b. Happy One.
   - ☐ c. Witch.

5. The aunt wanted Nicholas to
   - ☐ a. call the neighbors.
   - ☐ b. fetch a ladder.
   - ☐ c. grab a rope.

Understanding the Passage

6. Nicholas was hiding in the
   - ☐ a. gooseberry garden.
   - ☐ b. lumber-room.
   - ☐ c. library.

7. While looking for Nicholas, his aunt
   - ☐ a. grew more and more upset.
   - ☐ b. laughed at his little joke.
   - ☐ c. began picking raspberries.

8. After hearing his aunt's cry, Nicholas
   - ☐ a. panicked.
   - ☐ b. showed no great concern.
   - ☐ c. locked himself in his room.

9. While in the rainwater tank, the aunt
   - ☐ a. was hidden from Nicholas's view.
   - ☐ b. seemed fairly comfortable.
   - ☐ c. began to speak in a strange voice.

10. Nicholas's question about the strawberry jam
    - ☐ a. was a test to see who was in the rainwater tank.
    - ☐ b. caused his aunt to throw things out of the tank.
    - ☐ c. was not answered by his aunt.

Rosemary Fell was not exactly beautiful. No, you couldn't have called her beautiful. Pretty? Well, if you took her to pieces, but why be so cruel as to take anyone to pieces? She was young, brilliant, extremely modern, exquisitely well dressed, amazingly well read in the newest of the new books, and her parties were the most delicious mixture of the really important people and artists—quaint creatures, discoveries of hers, some of them too terrifying for words, but others quite presentable and amusing.

Rosemary had been married two years. She had a duck of a boy. No, not Peter—Michael. And her husband absolutely adored her. They were rich, really rich, not just comfortably well-off, which is odious and stuffy and sounds like one's grandparents. But if Rosemary wanted to shop she would go to Paris as you and I would go to Bond Street. If she wanted to buy flowers, the car pulled up at that perfect shop in Regent Street, and Rosemary inside the the shop just gazed in her dazzled, rather exotic way, and said: "I want those and those and those. Give me four bunches of those, and that jar of roses. Yes, I'll have all the roses in the jar. No, no lilac. I hate lilac. It's got no shape." The attendant bowed and put the lilac out of sight, as though this was only too true; lilac was dreadfully shapeless. "Give me those stumpy little tulips. Those red and white ones." And she was followed to the car by a thin shopgirl staggering under an immense white paper armful that looked like a baby in long clothes.

One winter afternoon she had been buying something in a little antique shop in Curzon Street. It was a shop she liked. For one thing, one usually had it to oneself. And then the man who kept it was ridiculously fond of serving her. He beamed whenever she came in. He clasped his hands; he was so gratified he could scarcely speak. Flattery, of course. All the same, there was something. . . .

"You see, madam," he would explain in his low respectful tones, "I love my things. I would rather not part with them than sell them to someone who does not appreciate them, who has not that fine feeling which is so rare." And, breathing deeply, he would unroll some tiny square of blue velvet.

Recalling Facts

1. Rosemary Fell was
   □ a. beautiful.
   □ b. rich.
   □ c. both a and b.

2. Rosemary had been married
   □ a. six months.
   □ b. two years.
   □ c. five years.

3. Rosemary hated
   □ a. roses.
   □ b. tulips.
   □ c. lilacs.

4. Rosemary's flowers were carried to her car by
   □ a. her mother.
   □ b. a shopgirl.
   □ c. Peter and Michael.

5. In the Curzon Street antique shop, Rosemary was usually
   □ a. the only customer.
   □ b. ignored by the owner.
   □ c. afraid of breaking things.

Understanding the Passage

6. Rosemary's parties were
   □ a. interesting.
   □ b. depressing.
   □ c. boring.

7. Rosemary never
   □ a. went to Paris.
   □ b. shopped in the afternoon.
   □ c. worried about money.

8. The attendant at the flower shop
   □ a. agreed with whatever Rosemary said.
   □ b. was allergic to lilac.
   □ c. always dressed in blue velvet.

9. Rosemary knew the man at the antique shop was trying to
   □ a. hide from her.
   □ b. cheat her.
   □ c. flatter her.

10. The man who ran the antique shop
    □ a. disliked Rosemary's hairstyle.
    □ b. valued Rosemary's business.
    □ c. did not trust Rosemary's husband.

I am too agitated to sleep. We have had such an adventure, such an agonizing experience. I fell asleep as soon as I had closed my diary. . . . Suddenly I became broad awake, and sat up, with a horrible sense of fear upon me, and of some feeling of emptiness around me. The room was dark, so I could not see Lucy's bed. I stole across and felt for her. The bed was empty. I lit a match and found that she was not in the room. The door was shut, but not locked, as I had left it. I feared to wake her mother, who has been more than usually ill lately, so I threw on some clothes and got ready to look for her. As I was leaving the room it struck me that the clothes she wore might give me some clue to her dreaming intention. Dressing gown would mean house; dress, outside. Dressing gown and dress were both in their places. "Thank God," I said to myself, "she cannot be far, as she is only in her nightdress." I ran downstairs and looked in the sitting room. Not there! Then I looked in all the other open rooms of the house, with an ever-growing fear chilling my heart. Finally I came to the hall door and found it open. It was not wide open, but the catch of the lock had not caught. The people of the house are careful to lock the door every night, so I feared that Lucy must have gone out as she was. There was no time to think of what might happen; a vague fear obscured all the details. I took a big, heavy shawl and ran out. The clock was striking one as I was in the Crescent, and there was not a soul in sight. I ran along the North Terrace, but could see no sign of the white figure which I expected. At the edge of the West Cliff above the pier I looked across the harbor to the East Cliff, in the hope or fear—I don't know which—of seeing Lucy in our favorite seat. There was a bright full moon, with heavy black, driving clouds, which threw the whole scene into a fleeting diorama of light and shade as they sailed across. For a moment or two I could see nothing, as the shadow of a cloud obscured St. Mary's Church.

Recalling Facts

1. After closing the diary, the narrator
   - □ a. took a walk.
   - □ b. ate a meal.
   - □ c. fell asleep.

2. In the dark room, the narrator could not see Lucy's
   - □ a. bed.
   - □ b. desk.
   - □ c. mirror.

3. Lucy's mother had
   - □ a. come to visit.
   - □ b. been rather ill.
   - □ c. just died.

4. The narrator tried to find Lucy in
   - □ a. the North Terrace.
   - □ b. Central Park.
   - □ c. West Cliff Heights.

5. The night was
   - □ a. perfectly clear.
   - □ b. partly cloudy.
   - □ c. totally overcast.

Understanding the Passage

6. To the narrator, the night's experience had been
   - □ a. unusual.
   - □ b. boring.
   - □ c. pleasurable.

7. The narrator awoke feeling
   - □ a. afraid.
   - □ b. refreshed.
   - □ c. relieved.

8. The narrator and Lucy
   - □ a. had the same fears.
   - □ b. slept in the same room.
   - □ c. read each other's diaries.

9. The "white figure" the narrator was looking for was Lucy in her
   - □ a. dressing gown.
   - □ b. dress.
   - □ c. nightdress.

10. The narrator thought Lucy
    - □ a. was nearby.
    - □ b. had drowned.
    - □ c. was lost.

Once again a pang of yearning for her mother to be near her today shot through Molly. She looked from her untamed man to the untamed desert of Wyoming, and the town where she was to take him as her wedded husband; but for his sake she would not let him guess her loneliness.

The Virginian sat on his horse Monte, considering the pistol. Then he showed her a rattlesnake coiled by the roots of some sagebrush. "Can I hit it?" he inquired.

"You don't often miss them," said Molly, striving to be cheerful.

"Well, I'm told getting married unstrings some men." The Virginian aimed, and the snake was shattered. "Maybe it's too early yet for the unstringing to begin!" And with some deliberation he sent three more bullets into the snake. "I reckon that's enough," said he.

"Was not the first one?"

"Oh, yes, for the snake." And then, with one leg crooked cowboy fashion across in front of his saddle horn, he cleaned his pistol, and replaced the empty cartridges.

Once more she ventured near the line of his reticence: "Has—has Trampas seen you much lately?"

"Why, no; not for a while; but I reckon he has not missed me."

The Virginian spoke this in his gentlest voice, but his rebuffed sweetheart turned her face away, and from her eyes she brushed a tear.

He reined his horse Monte beside her, and upon her cheek she felt his kiss. "You are not the only mind reader," said he, very tenderly. And at this she clung to him, and laid her head upon his breast. "I had been thinking," he went on, "that the way our marriage is to be was the most beautiful way."

"It is the most beautiful," she murmured.

The Virginian slowly spoke out his thought, as if she had not said this. "No folks to stare, no fuss, no jokes and ribbons and best bonnets, no public eye nor talkin' of tongues when most you want to hear nothing and say nothing. Just the Bishop of Wyoming to join us, and not even him after we're once joined. I did think that would be the perfect way to get married."

He paused again, and she made no rejoinder.

"But we have left out your mother."

She looked in his face with quick astonishment. It was as if his spirit had heard the cry of her spirit.

Recalling Facts

1. Molly missed her
   - ☐ a. husband.
   - ☐ b. children.
   - ☐ c. mother.

2. Molly was about to
   - ☐ a. leave the Virginian.
   - ☐ b. get married.
   - ☐ c. write her mother.

3. The Virginian's horse was named
   - ☐ a. Monte.
   - ☐ b. Wyoming.
   - ☐ c. Trampas.

4. The Virginian shot the snake
   - ☐ a. twice.
   - ☐ b. three times.
   - ☐ c. four times.

5. The Virginian said that he did not think he was missed by
   - ☐ a. Trampas.
   - ☐ b. the Bishop of Wyoming.
   - ☐ c. Molly.

Understanding the Passage

6. In this passage, Molly
   - ☐ a. did not appear to be very happy.
   - ☐ b. was eagerly anticipating her new life.
   - ☐ c. showed how much she distrusted the Virginian.

7. The Virginian was an excellent
   - ☐ a. animal tamer.
   - ☐ b. marksman.
   - ☐ c. carpenter.

8. Molly felt that the snake was
   - ☐ a. going to strike at her.
   - ☐ b. too small for the Virginian to shoot.
   - ☐ c. dead after the first shot.

9. The Virginian tried to
   - ☐ a. frighten Molly.
   - ☐ b. reassure Molly.
   - ☐ c. humor Molly.

10. The Virginian was
    - ☐ a. aware of Molly's unspoken thoughts.
    - ☐ b. not on speaking terms with Molly's mother.
    - ☐ c. being hunted by Trampas.

At eight o'clock the next morning, a faint kind of dawn of day awoke us. The thousand and one prisms of the lava collected the light as it passed, and brought it to us like a shower of sparks.

We were able with ease to see objects around us.

"Well, Harry, my boy," cried the delighted Professor, rubbing his hands together, "what say you now? Did you ever pass a more tranquil night in our house in the König Strasse? No deafening sounds of cartwheels, no cries of hawkers, no bad language from boatmen or watermen!"

"Well, uncle, we are quiet at the bottom of this well; but to me there is something terrible in this calm."

"Why," said the Professor, hotly, "one would say you were already beginning to be afraid. How will you get on presently? Do you know that, as yet, we have not penetrated one inch into the bowels of the earth?"

"What do you mean, sir?" was my bewildered reply.

"I mean to say that we have only just reached the soil of the island itself. This long vertical tube, which begins at the bottom of the crater of Sneffels, ceases here just about on a level with the sea."

"Are you sure, sir?"

"Quite sure. Consult the barometer."

It was quite true that the mercury, after rising gradually in the instrument, as long as our descent was taking place, had stopped precisely at twenty-nine degrees.

"You perceive," said the Professor, "we have as yet only to endure the pressure of air. I am curious to replace the barometer by the manometer."

The barometer, in fact, was about to become useless—as soon as the weight of the air was greater than what was calculated as above the level of the ocean.

"But," said I, "is it not very much to be feared that this growing pressure may in the end turn out very painful?"

"No," said he. "We shall descend very slowly. Our lungs will be gradually accustomed to breathe compressed air. It is well known that aëronauts have gone so high as to be nearly without air at all. Should we not accustom ourselves to breathe when we have, say, a little too much of it? For myself, I am certain I shall prefer it. Let us not lose a moment. Where is the packet which preceded us in our descent?"

Recalling Facts

1. When dawn came the Professor was
   - ☐ a. depressed.
   - ☐ b. frightened.
   - ☐ c. delighted.

2. The Professor and Harry had just reached
   - ☐ a. the center of the earth.
   - ☐ b. the top of Sneffels.
   - ☐ c. sea level.

3. The Professor asked Harry to check his
   - ☐ a. barometer.
   - ☐ b. thermometer.
   - ☐ c. manometer.

4. The Professor was eager to start using a
   - ☐ a. manometer.
   - ☐ b. odometer.
   - ☐ c. sextant.

5. Harry worried about
   - ☐ a. finding a way out.
   - ☐ b. the increasing air pressure.
   - ☐ c. the Professor's health.

Understanding the Passage

6. The Professor and Harry had just
   - ☐ a. fallen into a deep pit.
   - ☐ b. spent a peaceful night.
   - ☐ c. ended a hard day.

7. The light collected by the lava came from
   - ☐ a. lanterns.
   - ☐ b. candles.
   - ☐ c. the sun.

8. Harry found the calm
   - ☐ a. reassuring.
   - ☐ b. unusual.
   - ☐ c. disturbing.

9. From the Professor's point of view, the journey
   - ☐ a. was extremely hazardous.
   - ☐ b. had just begun.
   - ☐ c. was nearly over.

10. The Professor appeared to be
    - ☐ a. in a hurry to move on.
    - ☐ b. deeply hurt by Harry's comments.
    - ☐ c. growing increasingly nervous.

You must know that in a village four leagues and a half from this inn, it so happened that one of the local officials, by the tricks and roguery of a servant girl of his (it's too long a tale to tell), lost a donkey. Although he did all he possibly could to find it, it was all to no purpose. A fortnight might have gone by, so the story goes, since the donkey had been missing, when, as the official who had lost it was standing in the plaza, another official of the same town said to him, "Pay me for good news, friend. Your ● donkey has turned up." "That I will, and well, friend," said the other; "but tell me, where has he turned up?" "In the forest," said the finder; "I saw him this morning without packsaddle or harness of any sort. He looked so lean that it went to one's heart to see him. I tried to drive him before me and bring him to you. But he is already so wild and shy that when I went near him he made off into the thickest part of the forest. If you have a mind that we two should go back and look for him, let me put up my ● donkey at my house and I'll be back at once." "You will be doing me a great kindness," said the owner of the donkey, "and I'll try to pay it back in the same coin." Well then, the two officials set off on foot, arm in arm for the forest. When they came to the place where they hoped to find the donkey, they could not spot him, nor was he to be seen anywhere about, search as they might. Seeing, then, that there was no sign of him, the official who ● had seen him said to the other, "Look here, friend. A plan has occurred to me, by which beyond a doubt, we shall manage to discover the animal, even if he is stowed away in the bowels of the earth, not to say the forest. Here it is. I can bray to perfection, and if you can ever so little, the thing's as good as done." "Ever so little did you say, friend?" said the other. "By God, I'll not give in to anybody, not even to the donkeys themselves." "We'll soon see," said the second official, "for my plan is that you should go to one side of the forest, and I the other. Every now and then you will bray and I will bray. It cannot be but that the donkey will hear us, and answer us if he is in the forest."

Recalling Facts

1. The man who lost the donkey was a
   - ☐ a. servant.
   - ☐ b. local official.
   - ☐ c. forester.

2. The second official claimed to have seen the donkey
   - ☐ a. in the center of town.
   - ☐ b. heading toward the plaza.
   - ☐ c. in the forest.

3. The second official said the donkey looked
   - ☐ a. lean.
   - ☐ b. happy.
   - ☐ c. sick.

4. The second official said he could
   - ☐ a. bray to perfection.
   - ☐ b. run faster than any donkey.
   - ☐ c. find anything in the forest.

5. The two officials went to look for the donkey
   - ☐ a. on horseback.
   - ☐ b. on foot.
   - ☐ c. at nightfall.

Understanding the Passage

6. The owner of the donkey wanted to
   - ☐ a. get his donkey back.
   - ☐ b. help the second official.
   - ☐ c. punish the servant girl.

7. The owner of the donkey was
   - ☐ a. furious with the other official.
   - ☐ b. the brother of the other official.
   - ☐ c. grateful for the other official's help.

8. The second official believed he had
   - ☐ a. harmed the donkey.
   - ☐ b. a good plan for catching the donkey.
   - ☐ c. become lost in the forest.

9. The lost donkey was becoming
   - ☐ a. less and less tame.
   - ☐ b. more and more friendly.
   - ☐ c. bigger and bigger.

10. The owner of the donkey believed he could
    - ☐ a. sue the servant who let the donkey escape.
    - ☐ b. imitate the sounds of a donkey.
    - ☐ c. not trust the second official.

One afternoon Frank and Gus found No. 11 on the sidetrack, puffing away as if enjoying a quiet smoke before starting. No cars were attached, and no driver was to be seen. Bill was off with the other men behind the station house, helping the expressman, whose horse had backed down a bank and upset the wagon.

"Good chance for a look at the old lady," said Frank, speaking of the engine as Bill did, and jumping aboard with great satisfaction, followed by Gus.

"I'd give ten dollars if I could run her up to the bend and back," he added, fondly touching the bright brass knobs and glancing at the fire with a critical eye.

"You couldn't do it alone," answered Gus, sitting down on the grimy little perch, willing to indulge his mate's weakness.

"Give me leave to try? Steam is up. I could do it as easy as not," and Frank put his hand on the throttle valve, as if daring Gus to give the word.

"Fire up and make her hum!" laughed Gus, quoting Bill's frequent order to his mate, but with no idea of being obeyed.

"All right! I'll just roll her up to the switch and back again. I've often done it with Bill." And Frank cautiously opened the throttle valve, threw back the lever, and the great thing moved with a throb and a puff.

"Steady, old fellow, or you'll come to grief. Here, don't open that!" shouted Gus, for just at that moment Joe appeared at the switch, looking ready for mischief.

"Wish he would; no train for twenty minutes, and we could run up to the bend as well as not," said Frank, getting excited with the sense of power. The monster obeyed his hand so entirely that it was impossible to resist prolonging the delight.

"By George, he has! Stop her! Back her! Hold on, Frank!" cried Gus, as Joe, only catching the words "Open that!" obeyed, without the least idea that they would dare to leave the siding.

But they did, for Frank rather lost his head for a minute, and out upon the main track rolled No. 11 as quietly as a well-trained horse taking a familiar road.

"Now you've done it! I'll give you a good thrashing when I get back!" roared Gus, shaking his fist as Joe, who stood staring, half-pleased, half-scared, at what he had done.

Recalling Facts

1. Frank and Gus found No. 11
   - ☐ a. on the main track.
   - ☐ b. on a sidetrack.
   - ☐ c. in the repair shed.

2. "The old lady" referred to
   - ☐ a. the train engine.
   - ☐ b. Bill's mother.
   - ☐ c. the station master.

3. Joe opened the
   - ☐ a. throttle valve.
   - ☐ b. lever.
   - ☐ c. switch.

4. Another train was not expected for
   - ☐ a. twenty minutes.
   - ☐ b. two days.
   - ☐ c. two hours.

5. Gus threatened to thrash
   - ☐ a. Joe.
   - ☐ b. Bill.
   - ☐ c. Frank.

Understanding the Passage

6. Bill apparently was
   - ☐ a. Frank's father.
   - ☐ b. the regular driver of No. 11.
   - ☐ c. the expressman.

7. Frank picked up the expression "the old lady" from
   - ☐ a. Bill.
   - ☐ b. Gus.
   - ☐ c. Joe.

8. The train's engine
   - ☐ a. needed to be fired up.
   - ☐ b. needed many repairs.
   - ☐ c. was ready to roll.

9. Frank had
   - ☐ a. made practice runs with Bill.
   - ☐ b. never been in the engine before.
   - ☐ c. experience running trains on the main track.

10. When Joe opened the switch, Gus was
    - ☐ a. laughing with delight.
    - ☐ b. surprised and angry.
    - ☐ c. embarrassed and nervous.

from **The Eustace Diamonds** *by Anthony Trollope*

The reader will perhaps remember that when Lizzie Eustace was told that her aunt was downstairs, Frank Greystock was with her, and that he promised to return on the following day to hear the result of the interview. Had Lady Linlithgow not come at that very moment Frank would probably have asked his rich cousin to be his wife. She had told him that she was unhappy, and after that what else could he have done but ask her to be his wife? The old Countess, however, arrived and interrupted him. He went away abruptly, promising to come on the morrow. But on the morrow he never came. It was a Friday, and Lizzie remained at home for him the whole morning. When four o'clock was passed she knew that he would be at the House. But still she did not stir. And she contrived that Miss Macnulty should be absent the entire day. Miss Macnulty was even made to go to the play by herself in the evening. But her absence was of no service. Frank Greystock came not, and at eleven at night Lizzie swore to herself that should he ever come again, he should come in vain.

Nevertheless, through the whole of Saturday she expected him with more or less of confidence, and on the Sunday morning she was still well inclined toward him. It might be that he would come on that day. She could understand that a man with his hands so full of business as were those of her Cousin Frank should find himself unable to keep an appointment. Nor would there be fair ground for anger with such a one, even should he forget an appointment. But surely he would come on the Sunday! She had been quite sure that the offer was about to be made when that old woman had come in and disturbed everything. Indeed, the offer had been all but made. She had felt the flutter, had asked herself the important question, and had answered it. She had told herself that the thing would do. Frank was not the exact hero that her fancy had painted, but he was sufficiently heroic. Everybody said that he would work his way up to the top and become a rich man. At any rate she had resolved—and then Lady Linlithgow had come in! Surely he would come on the Sunday.

Recalling Facts

1. Frank left Lizzie when her
   - ☐ a. sister came.
   - ☐ b. aunt came.
   - ☐ c. mother came.

2. Lizzie had told Frank that she was
   - ☐ a. unhappy.
   - ☐ b. wealthy.
   - ☐ c. nervous.

3. Frank promised to come back
   - ☐ a. in a week.
   - ☐ b. in a few days.
   - ☐ c. the next day.

4. In her mind, Lizzie had agreed to become Frank's
   - ☐ a. business partner.
   - ☐ b. advisor.
   - ☐ c. wife.

5. Everyone thought that Frank would become
   - ☐ a. rich.
   - ☐ b. penniless.
   - ☐ c. famous.

Understanding the Passage

6. Lizzie was
   - ☐ a. upset to be interrupted by Lady Linlithgow.
   - ☐ b. happy to see Lady Linlithgow.
   - ☐ c. anxious to get rid of Frank.

7. On Friday, Lizzie wanted to
   - ☐ a. spend the day with Miss Macnulty.
   - ☐ b. be alone with Frank.
   - ☐ c. visit Lady Linlithgow.

8. Lizzie realized that Frank was
   - ☐ a. a liar.
   - ☐ b. seeing another woman.
   - ☐ c. a busy man.

9. To Lizzie, Frank appeared to be the
   - ☐ a. best man available.
   - ☐ b. answer to her wildest dreams.
   - ☐ c. only man she could attract.

10. Lizzie's mood slowly shifted to one of
   - ☐ a. great relief.
   - ☐ b. high anxiety.
   - ☐ c. personal guilt.

The Queen ordered Peter Pan to kneel, and then said that for playing so beautifully she would give him the wish of his heart. Then the fairies all gathered round Peter to hear what was the wish of his heart, but for a long time he hesitated, not being certain what it was himself.

"If I chose to go back to mother," he asked at last, "could you give me that wish?"

Now this question vexed them, for were he to return to his mother they should lose his music, so the Queen tilted her nose and said, "Pooh, ask for a much bigger wish than that."

"Is that quite a little wish?" he asked.

"As little as this," the Queen answered, putting her hands near each other.

"What size is a big wish?" he asked.

She measured it off on her skirt and it was a very handsome length.

Then Peter reflected and said, "Well, then, I think I shall have two little wishes instead of one big one."

Of course, the fairies had to agree, though his cleverness rather shocked them, and he said that his first wish was to go to his mother, but with the right to return to the Gardens if he found her disappointing. His second wish he would hold in reserve.

They tried to dissuade him, and even put obstacles in the way.

"I can give you the power to fly to her house," the Queen said, "but I can't open the door for you."

"The window I flew out at will be open," Peter said confidently. "Mother always keeps it open in the hope that I may fly back."

"How do you know?" they asked, quite surprised, and, really, Peter could not explain how he knew.

"I just do know," he said.

So as he persisted in his wish, they had to grant it. They all tickled him on the shoulder. Soon he felt a funny itching in that part and then up he rose higher and higher and flew away out of the Gardens.

It was so delicious that instead of flying straight to his old home he skipped away over St. Paul's to the Crystal Palace and back by the river and Regent's Park, and by the time he reached his mother's window he had quite made up his mind that his second wish would be to become a bird.

Recalling Facts

1. The fairies did not want to lose Peter Pan's
   - ☐ a. music.
   - ☐ b. gardens.
   - ☐ c. company.

2. The Queen said that Peter's wish to see his mother was
   - ☐ a. too small.
   - ☐ b. just right.
   - ☐ c. too big.

3. Peter's first wish was to
   - ☐ a. have many wishes.
   - ☐ b. visit his mother.
   - ☐ c. see the Gardens.

4. The fairies granted Peter his wish by
   - ☐ a. tickling his shoulder.
   - ☐ b. sprinkling magic powder on him.
   - ☐ c. saying special words.

5. Peter's second wish was to become a
   - ☐ a. fairy.
   - ☐ b. horse.
   - ☐ c. bird.

Understanding the Passage

6. When first told he could have any wish, Peter
   - ☐ a. knew exactly what he wanted.
   - ☐ b. jumped for joy.
   - ☐ c. was unsure what to ask for.

7. The Queen wanted Peter to wish for something that would
   - ☐ a. keep him in the Gardens.
   - ☐ b. please his mother.
   - ☐ c. be difficult to grant.

8. The fairies were
   - ☐ a. deceitful.
   - ☐ b. honorable.
   - ☐ c. powerless.

9. The fairies gave Peter the power to
   - ☐ a. think.
   - ☐ b. love.
   - ☐ c. fly.

10. Peter thought that when he got home, the window would be
    - ☐ a. closed.
    - ☐ b. open.
    - ☐ c. broken.

Experience teaches me that the going astray of the best laid plans includes railroads.

My first hint came from the sleeping car porter.

"Eight o'clock, sir. Last berth occupied."

More positive data proceeded from the conductor, who clicked a punch under my nose and blurted out, "Tickets!"

I fumbled mechanically under my pillow, and remembering, said sleepily, "Gave them to you last night."

"Not to me. Want your tickets for Richmond."

I sat up. Whole rows of people up and dressed for all day were quietly and contentedly occupying their seats. Every berth was swept away. My curtains alone dangled from the continuous brass rod, every eye in the car being fastened on my traveling bedroom.

"I am not going to Richmond. I get off at Washington."

"Wrong car, sir. Left Washington two hours ago."

"Stop at the next station," I gasped, grabbing my coat.

The conductor peered through the car window, pulled the bell rope, and called out, "All out for Squantico!" and the next moment I was shivering in a pool of snow and water, my bag bottom side up, the rear of the retreating train filling a distant cut.

A man in a fur hat regarded me a moment, picked up a mail pouch from a half-melted snowbank, and preceded me up a muddy road flanked by a worm fence. I overtook him, and added my bag to his load.

"When can I get back to Washington?"

"Ten minutes past two."

I made a hurried calculation. Six hours! What could a man do with six hours in a hole like this? Before I had turned the road I had learned all that could possibly interest me: the hotel was closed, Colonel Jarvis kept a store third house from the corner, and Mrs. Jarvis could get me a breakfast.

It was not a cheery morning to land anywhere. January thaw mornings never are. A drizzling rain saturated everything. A steaming fog hung over the low country, drifted out over the river, and made ghosts of the piles of an unfinished dock. The mud was inches deep under the snow, which lay sprawling out in patches covering the ground like a worn out coat. A dozen of cheaply constructed houses and stores built of wood fronted on one side of a broad road. Opposite the group was a great barn of a building, with its doors and lower windows boarded up. This was the hotel.

*Reading Time*_____   *Comprehension Score*_____   *Words per Minute*_____

Recalling Facts

1. The narrator (the person telling this story) claimed he gave the conductor his tickets
   □ a. yesterday afternoon.
   □ b. last night.
   □ c. earlier that morning.

2. The conductor wanted to see the narrator's tickets to
   □ a. Richmond.
   □ b. Washington.
   □ c. Squantico.

3. The scene took place in
   □ a. October.
   □ b. January.
   □ c. April.

4. In Squantico, Colonel Jarvis ran a
   □ a. farm.
   □ b. store.
   □ c. hotel.

5. The hotel looked like
   □ a. a palace.
   □ b. an old factory.
   □ c. a great barn.

Understanding the Passage

6. Apparently, the narrator
   □ a. wanted to see Squantico.
   □ b. slept through his stop.
   □ c. knew the conductor.

7. The other passengers on the train
   □ a. were curious about the narrator's problem.
   □ b. hardly noticed the narrator.
   □ c. almost threw the narrator off the train.

8. The narrator viewed Squantico with
   □ a. scorn.
   □ b. interest.
   □ c. amazement.

9. The narrator's mood was made worse by
   □ a. the weather.
   □ b. Mrs. Jarvis's cooking.
   □ c. Squantico's high prices.

10. Squantico appeared to be a
    □ a. deserted ghost town.
    □ b. small and poor town.
    □ c. nice place to spend time.

Aunt Sarah had the air of a woman who knew her own mind and commonly had her own way.

"Well, Esther, I am glad to see you taking George to church. Has he behaved himself?"

"You are wrong again, Aunt Sarah," said George; "it is I who have been taking Esther to church. I thought it was worth seeing."

"Church is always worth seeing, George, and I hope your friend Mr. Hazard's sermon has done you good."

"It did me good to see Wharton there," answered George. "He looked as though it were a first representation, and he were in a stage box. Hazard and he ought to have appeared before the curtain, hand in hand, and made little speeches. I felt like calling them out."

"What did you think of it, Esther?" asked her aunt.

"I thought it very entertaining, Aunt Sarah. I felt like a butterfly in a tulip bed. Mr. Hazard's eyes are wonderful."

"I shall never get you two to be reverential," said her aunt sternly. "It was the best sermon I ever heard, and I would like to hear you answer it, George, and make your answer as little scientific as you can."

"Aunt Sarah, I never answered anyone in my life, not even you, or Esther, or the man who said that my fossil bird was a crocodile. Why do you want me to answer him?"

"Because I don't believe you can."

"I can't. I am a professor of paleontology at the college, and I answer questions about bones. You must get my colleague who does the metaphysics to answer Hazard's sermon. Hazard and I have had it out fifty times, and discussed the whole subject till night reeled, but we never got within shouting distance of each other. He might as well have stood on the earth, and I on the nearest planet, and bawled across. So we have given it up."

"You mean that you were beaten," rejoined his aunt. "I am glad you feel it, though I always knew it was so. After all, Mr. Hazard has got more saints on his church walls than he will ever see in his audience, though not such pretty ones. I never saw so many lovely faces and dresses together. Esther, how is your father today?"

"Not very well, aunt. He wants to see you. Come home with us and help us to amuse him."

Recalling Facts

1. Aunt Sarah was glad
   that Esther and George
   had been to
   □ a. court.
   □ b. church.
   □ c. school.

2. Esther was most impressed by
   Mr. Hazard's
   □ a. eyes.
   □ b. height.
   □ c. intellect.

3. George was a professor of
   □ a. philosophy.
   □ b. paleontology.
   □ c. metaphysics.

4. Aunt Sarah said it was
   hopeless to get Esther and
   George to be more
   □ a. reverential.
   □ b. scientific.
   □ c. thrifty.

5. George no longer wanted
   to debate
   □ a. politics.
   □ b. economics.
   □ c. religion.

Understanding the Passage

6. George and Esther were
   □ a. not devout churchgoers.
   □ b. very cruel to Aunt
      Sarah.
   □ c. upset with Mr. Hazard.

7. Aunt Sarah appeared to be
   □ a. disappointed with
      Mr. Hazard.
   □ b. upset with George
      and Esther.
   □ c. concerned about
      Wharton's health.

8. Aunt Sarah didn't think
   that George
   □ a. could win a debate with
      Mr. Hazard.
   □ b. was happy with Esther.
   □ c. both a and b.

9. The discussions between
   George and Mr. Hazard had
   ended with
   □ a. George winning.
   □ b. the two men becoming
      friendly.
   □ c. neither side giving in to
      the other.

10. Aunt Sarah felt Mr.
    Hazard had
    □ a. lost interest in religion.
    □ b. defeated George.
    □ c. forgotten how to argue.

"But what I wanted to ask you was, won't you take me to call on Mr. Toad? I've heard so much about him," said the Mole, "and I do so want to make his acquaintance."

"Why, certainly," said the good-natured Rat, jumping to his feet. "Get the boat out, and we'll paddle up there at once. It's never the wrong time to call on Toad. Early or late he's always the same fellow. Always good-tempered, always glad to see you, always sorry when you go!"

"He must be a very nice animal," observed the Mole, as he got into the boat and took the sculls, while the Rat settled himself comfortably in the stern.

"He is indeed the best of animals," replied Rat. "So simple, so good-natured, and so affectionate. Perhaps he's not very clever—we can't all be geniuses; and it may be that he is both boastful and conceited. But he has got some great qualities, has Toady."

Rounding a bend in the river, they came in sight of a handsome, dignified old house of mellowed red brick, with well-kept lawns reaching down to the water's edge.

"There's Toad Hall," said the Rat; "and that creek on the left, where the notice board says, 'Private. No landing allowed,' leads to his boathouse, where we'll leave the boat. The stables are over there to the right. That's the banqueting hall you're looking at now—very old, that is. Toad is rather rich, you know, and this is really one of the nicest houses in these parts, though we never admit as much to Toad."

They glided up the creek, and the Mole shipped his sculls as they passed into the shadows of a large boathouse. Here they saw many handsome boats, slung from the crossbeams or hauled up on a slip, but none in the water; and the place had an unused and a deserted air.

The Rat looked around him. "I understand," said he. "Boating is played out. He's tired of it, and done with it. I wonder what new fad he has taken up now? Come along and let's look him up. We shall hear all about it quite soon enough."

They disembarked, and strolled across the gay flower-decked lawns in search of Toad, whom they presently happened upon resting in a wicker garden chair, with a preoccupied expression of face, and a large map spread out on his knees.

"Hooray!" Toad cried.

Recalling Facts

1. The Rat and the Mole wanted to visit
   - ☐ a. Frog.
   - ☐ b. Toad.
   - ☐ c. Tadpole.

2. The Rat and the Mole traveled by
   - ☐ a. steamer.
   - ☐ b. canoe.
   - ☐ c. boat.

3. The Toad was known for being
   - ☐ a. very clever.
   - ☐ b. good-natured.
   - ☐ c. both a and b.

4. The Toad's house was made out of
   - ☐ a. red brick.
   - ☐ b. dark wood.
   - ☐ c. white stone.

5. When the Rat and the Mole arrived, Toad had
   - ☐ a. a map spread out on his knees.
   - ☐ b. just finished painting his boat.
   - ☐ c. just begun to work in his garden.

Understanding the Passage

6. Toad was always
   - ☐ a. ill-tempered.
   - ☐ b. a gracious host.
   - ☐ c. out boating.

7. Apparently, the Toad had
   - ☐ a. some small character flaws.
   - ☐ b. a large vacation home.
   - ☐ c. very little free time.

8. The Toad had given up
   - ☐ a. hosting.
   - ☐ b. gardening.
   - ☐ c. boating.

9. The Mole had never
   - ☐ a. met Mr. Toad.
   - ☐ b. been boating with the Rat.
   - ☐ c. ridden in a boat before.

10. The Rat
   - ☐ a. was puzzled by Mr. Toad.
   - ☐ b. knew Mr. Toad well.
   - ☐ c. avoided visiting Mr. Toad.

It was in the full flush of April that a telegram came summoning Charlie home at once. Terror seized her like some tangible thing. She feared someone was dead.

Her father had been hurt, they told her. Not fatally, but he wanted her.

It was one of those terrible catastrophes which seem so impossible, so uncalled for when they come home to us; they stun us with grief and regret. There had been an accident at the sugar mill; a bit of perilous repairing in which he chose to assume the risk rather than expose others to danger. It was hard to say what had happened to him. He was alive; that was all, but torn, maimed, and unconscious. The surgeon, who was coming as fast as steam and the iron wheels could bring him, would tell them more of it. The surgeon was on the train with Charlie and so was the professional nurse. They seemed to her like monsters; because he read a newspaper and conversed with the conductor about crops and the weather; and the other, demure in her grey dress and close bonnet, displayed an interest in a group of children who were traveling with their mother.

Charlie could not speak. Her brain was confused with horror and her thoughts were beyond control. Everything had lost significance but her grief. Nothing was real but her despair. Emotion stupefied her when she thought that he would not be there at the station waiting for her with outstretched arms. She would perhaps never see him again as he had been that day at the lake, robust and beautiful, clasping her with loving arms when he said good-bye in the soft twilight. She became keenly conscious of the rhythm of the iron wheels. They seemed to mock her while keeping time to the throbbing in her head and bosom.

There was a hush upon the whole plantation. Silent embraces, serious faces, and tearful eyes greeted her. It seemed inexpressibly hard that she should be kept from him while the surgeon and the nurse were hurried to his side. A physician was already there, and so was Mr. Gus.

During the hour or more that followed, Charlie sat alone on the upper gallery. Madame Philomel with Julia and Amanda were indoors praying upon their knees. The others were speechless with worry. Charlie alone was quiet and dull.

Recalling Facts

1. Charlie headed home after
   - ☐ a. losing her job.
   - ☐ b. being injured in an accident.
   - ☐ c. receiving a telegram.

2. Charlie's father had been working
   - ☐ a. on a farm.
   - ☐ b. on a printing press.
   - ☐ c. at a sugar mill.

3. On the train home, Charlie saw
   - ☐ a. Mr. Gus.
   - ☐ b. her father's boss.
   - ☐ c. the surgeon.

4. Charlie saw the surgeon
   - ☐ a. reading the newspaper.
   - ☐ b. playing with some children.
   - ☐ c. sitting without speaking.

5. After arriving at the plantation, Charlie
   - ☐ a. went inside and prayed.
   - ☐ b. waited on the upper gallery.
   - ☐ c. went directly to her father.

Understanding the Passage

6. The news of the accident
   - ☐ a. shocked Charlie.
   - ☐ b. annoyed Charlie.
   - ☐ c. confused Charlie.

7. Charlie expected the surgeon and the nurse to be
   - ☐ a. more cheerful.
   - ☐ b. somewhat distressed.
   - ☐ c. dressed in black.

8. Charlie had
   - ☐ a. no memories of her father.
   - ☐ b. bad memories of her father.
   - ☐ c. fond memories of her father.

9. The people at the plantation seemed
   - ☐ a. preoccupied with the harvest.
   - ☐ b. nervous about seeing Charlie.
   - ☐ c. worried about Charlie's father.

10. The professional nurse came to
    - ☐ a. take care of Charlie.
    - ☐ b. supervise the local nurse.
    - ☐ c. assist the surgeon.

"There is a cottage not far from our house. There is just a field between us, but to reach it you have to go along the road and then turn down a lane. Just beyond it is a nice little grove of Scotch firs, and I used to be very fond of strolling down there, for trees are always a neighborly kind of thing. The cottage had been standing empty this eight months. It was a pity, for it was a pretty two-storied place, with an old-fashioned porch and a honeysuckle about it. I have stood many a time and thought what a neat little homestead it would make.

"Well, last Monday evening I was taking a stroll down that way when I met an empty van coming up the lane and saw a pile of carpets and things lying about on the grass plot beside the porch. It was clear that the cottage had at last been let. I walked past it, and then stopping, as an idle man might, I ran my eye over it and wondered what sort of folk they were who had come to live so near us. And as I looked I suddenly became aware that a face was watching me out of one of the upper windows.

"I don't know what there was about that face, Mr. Holmes, but it seemed to send a chill right down my back. I was some little way off, so that I could not make out the features. But there was something unnatural and inhuman about the face. That was the impression that I had, and I moved quickly forward to get a nearer view of the person who was watching me. But as I did so the face suddenly disappeared, so suddenly that it seemed to have been plucked away into the darkness of the room. I stood for five minutes thinking the business over and trying to analyze my impressions. I could not tell if the face was that of a man or a woman. It had been too far from me for that. But its color was what had impressed me most. It was a livid chalky white, and with something set and rigid about it which was shockingly unnatural. So disturbed was I that I determined to see a little more of the new inmates of the cottage. I approached and knocked at the door."

Recalling Facts

1. The narrator loved to
   - ☐ a. climb mountains.
   - ☐ b. walk along the shore.
   - ☐ c. stroll through the woods.

2. The cottage had been empty for
   - ☐ a. two years.
   - ☐ b. eight months.
   - ☐ c. several weeks.

3. Beside the porch the narrator saw a pile of
   - ☐ a. carpets.
   - ☐ b. toys.
   - ☐ c. leaves.

4. In this passage, the narrator was talking to
   - ☐ a. the man in the window.
   - ☐ b. Mr. Holmes.
   - ☐ c. himself.

5. The face in the window was
   - ☐ a. chalky white.
   - ☐ b. terror stricken.
   - ☐ c. a young child's.

Understanding the Passage

6. The narrator lived
   - ☐ a. in the cottage.
   - ☐ b. not far from the cottage.
   - ☐ c. in another country.

7. The narrator thought that the cottage
   - ☐ a. should be torn down.
   - ☐ b. was rather ugly.
   - ☐ c. would make a nice home for someone.

8. The face in the window
   - ☐ a. bothered the narrator.
   - ☐ b. delighted the narrator.
   - ☐ c. shamed the narrator.

9. The face in the window
   - ☐ a. sparked the narrator's curiosity.
   - ☐ b. seemed warm and friendly.
   - ☐ c. both a and b.

10. The narrator
   - ☐ a. seemed to recognize the face.
   - ☐ b. decided to mind his own business.
   - ☐ c. wanted to get a closer look.

A seal did not go very far, for each mouth in the little village had a right to be filled. Neither bone, hide, nor sinew was wasted. Even the dogs' meat was taken for human use. Amoraq fed the team of dogs with pieces of old summer skin tents raked out from under the sleeping bench, and they howled and howled again, and waked to howl hungrily. One could tell by the soapstone lamps in the huts that famine was near. In the good seasons, when blubber was plentiful, the light in the boat-shaped lamps would be two feet high—cheerful, oily, and yellow. Now it was a bare six inches. Amoraq carefully pricked down the moss wick, when an unwatched flame brightened for a moment, and the eyes of all the family followed her hand. The horror of famine up there in the great cold is not so much dying, as dying in the dark. All the Inuit dread the dark that presses on them without a break for six months in each year. When the lamps are low in the houses the minds of people begin to be shaken and confused.

But worse was to come.

The underfed dogs snapped and growled in the passages. They glared at the cold stars, and snuffed into the bitter wind, night after night. When they stopped howling the silence fell down again as solid and as heavy as a snowdrift against a door. Then men could hear the beating of their blood in the thin passages of the ear, and the thumping of their own hearts, that sounded as loud as the noise of sorcerers' drums beaten across the snow. One night Kotuko the dog, who had been unusually sullen in harness, leaped up and pushed his head against Kotuko the boy's knee. Kotuko patted him. But the dog still pushed blindly forward, fawning. Then Kadlu waked, and gripped the heavy wolflike head, and stared into the glassy eyes. The dog whimpered and shivered between Kadlu's knees. The hair rose about his neck, and he growled as though a stranger were at the door. Then he barked joyously, and rolled on the ground, and bit at Kotuko's boot like a puppy.

"What is it?" said Kotuko; for he was beginning to be afraid.

"The sickness," Kadlu answered. "It is the dog sickness." Kotuko the dog lifted his nose and howled and howled again.

Recalling Facts

1. Amoraq fed the dogs with
   - ☐ a. scraps left over from the family's meal.
   - ☐ b. blubber and seal meat.
   - ☐ c. old summer skin tents.

2. The Inuit dreaded the
   - ☐ a. wolves.
   - ☐ b. dark.
   - ☐ c. rain.

3. When famine was near, the light in the soapstone lamps was
   - ☐ a. two feet high.
   - ☐ b. six inches high.
   - ☐ c. extinguished.

4. Lately, Kotuko the dog had been unusually
   - ☐ a. sullen.
   - ☐ b. agreeable.
   - ☐ c. strong.

5. Kadlu thought that Kotuko the dog had
   - ☐ a. worms.
   - ☐ b. the dog sickness.
   - ☐ c. food poisoning.

Understanding the Passage

6. Kadlu knew how to handle
   - ☐ a. sick dogs.
   - ☐ b. wounded seals.
   - ☐ c. babies.

7. The Inuit were often at the mercy of
   - ☐ a. sled dogs.
   - ☐ b. nature.
   - ☐ c. local merchants.

8. Kotuko the dog's strange behavior
   - ☐ a. alarmed Kotuko the boy.
   - ☐ b. puzzled Kadlu.
   - ☐ c. both a and b.

9. The dogs often howled to show their
   - ☐ a. contentedness.
   - ☐ b. loneliness.
   - ☐ c. hunger.

10. When the dogs were not howling,
    - ☐ a. the Inuit chanted to keep away the silence.
    - ☐ b. the crying of seals could be heard.
    - ☐ c. silence dominated the area.

I stole home by the garden and climbed in at the window of a back parlor on the ground floor. The room above was my aunt's bedchamber, and the moment I was inside the house I heard moans. My aunt was a quiet, composed woman. I could not imagine that the loud sobbing and moaning came from her, and I ran down terrified into the kitchen to ask the servants who was crying so violently in my aunt's room.

I found the housemaid and the cook talking together in whispers with serious faces. They started when they saw me as if I had been a grown-up master who had caught them neglecting their work.

"He's too young to feel it much," I heard one say to the other. "So far as he is concerned, it seems like a mercy that it happened no later."

In a few minutes they had told me the worst. It was indeed my aunt who had been crying in the bedroom. Caroline was dead.

I felt the blow more severely than the servants or anyone else about me supposed. Still I was a child in years, and I had the blessed elasticity of a child's nature. If I had been older, I might have been too much absorbed in grief to observe my aunt so closely as I did when she was composed enough to see me later in the day.

I was not surprised by the swollen state of her eyes, the paleness of her cheeks, or the fresh burst of tears that came from her when she took me in her arms at meeting. But I was amazed by the look of terror that I detected in her face. It was natural enough that she should grieve and weep over my sister's death. But why should she have that frightened look as if some other catastrophe had happened?

I asked if there was any more dreadful news from home besides the news of Caroline's death. My aunt said no in a strange, stifled voice, and suddenly turned her face from me. Was my father dead? No. My mother? No. Uncle George? My aunt trembled all over as she said no to that also, and bade me cease asking any more questions. She was not fit to bear them yet, she said, and signed to the servant to lead me out of the room.

Recalling Facts

1. The moment the narrator entered the house, he heard
   - ☐ a. glass breaking.
   - ☐ b. music.
   - ☐ c. moans.

2. The narrator heard the news from the housemaid and the
   - ☐ a. cook.
   - ☐ b. gardener.
   - ☐ c. nanny.

3. The dead person was
   - ☐ a. not identified.
   - ☐ b. Uncle George.
   - ☐ c. the narrator's sister.

4. The narrator was amazed by his aunt's look of
   - ☐ a. grief.
   - ☐ b. terror.
   - ☐ c. relief.

5. The narrator's aunt begged him
   - ☐ a. to get some sleep.
   - ☐ b. not to ask any more questions.
   - ☐ c. to give her a hug.

Understanding the Passage

6. When the narrator first heard the sobs, he did not know
   - ☐ a. what caused them.
   - ☐ b. where they were coming from.
   - ☐ c. both a and b.

7. The narrator was blessed with
   - ☐ a. inexperience.
   - ☐ b. intelligence.
   - ☐ c. youth.

8. When the narrator entered the kitchen, the servants
   - ☐ a. refused to talk to him.
   - ☐ b. told him the truth.
   - ☐ c. pretended nothing was wrong.

9. The narrator appeared to be
   - ☐ a. an unfeeling brother.
   - ☐ b. a keen observer.
   - ☐ c. easily terrified.

10. The narrator was most surprised by
    - ☐ a. the whispers of the servants.
    - ☐ b. the cause of Caroline's death.
    - ☐ c. his aunt's behavior.

from **William Tell** *by Horace Elisha Scudder*

In the marketplace of Altorf, a Swiss town, Gessler set up a tall pole, like a liberty pole. But on top of this pole he placed his hat, and, just as in the city a gilt crown on some high point was the sign of the emperor's power, so this hat was to be the sign of Gessler's power. He bade that every Swiss man, woman, or child who passed by the pole should bow to the hat. In this way they were to show their respect for him.

From one of the mountain homes near Altorf there came into the marketplace one day a tall, strong man named William Tell. He was a famous archer, for it was in the days before the mountaineers carried guns, and he was wont to shoot bears and wild goats and wolves with his bow and arrows.

He had with him his little son, and they walked across the marketplace. But when they passed the pole, Tell never bent his head. He stood as straight as a mountain pine.

There were servants and spies of Gessler in the marketplace, and they at once told the tyrant how Tell had defied him. Gessler commanded the Swiss to be brought before him, and he came, leading by the hand his little son.

"They tell me you shoot well," said the tyrant. "You shall not be punished. Instead you shall give me a sign of your skill. Your boy is no doubt made of the same stuff you are. Let him stand yonder a hundred paces off. Place an apple on his head, and do you stand here and pierce the apple with an arrow from your quiver."

All the people about turned pale with fear, and fathers who had their sons with them held them fast, as if Gessler meant to take them from them. But Tell looked Gessler full in the face, and drew two arrows from his quiver.

"Go yonder," he said to the lad, and he saw him led away by two servants of Gessler, who paced a hundred steps, and then placed an apple on the boy's head. They had some pity for Tell in their hearts, and so they had made the boy stand with his back to his father.

"Face this way," rang out Tell's clear voice, and the boy, quick to obey, turned and stood facing his father.

Recalling Facts

1. On top of the pole, Gessler placed his
   - ☐ a. gilt crown.
   - ☐ b. hat.
   - ☐ c. family flag.

2. Every Swiss who passed the pole was supposed to
   - ☐ a. kiss the ground.
   - ☐ b. salute.
   - ☐ c. bow.

3. The pole was set up
   - ☐ a. in the marketplace.
   - ☐ b. in front of Gessler's castle.
   - ☐ c. on the outskirts of Altorf.

4. Gessler told Tell that he would
   - ☐ a. not be punished if he proved his skill.
   - ☐ b. go to prison when he finished eating.
   - ☐ c. have to split an apple with an axe.

5. One of Gessler's servants
   - ☐ a. made the boy face his father.
   - ☐ b. placed a blindfold over the boy's eyes.
   - ☐ c. placed an apple on the boy's head.

Understanding the Passage

6. Gessler wanted the people to
   - ☐ a. love him.
   - ☐ b. fear him.
   - ☐ c. leave him alone.

7. Tell's reputation as an archer was
   - ☐ a. well known.
   - ☐ b. a family secret.
   - ☐ c. greatly exaggerated.

8. Tell apparently
   - ☐ a. did not like his son.
   - ☐ b. did not know how to shoot arrows.
   - ☐ c. had great confidence in his own ability.

9. Other fathers
   - ☐ a. enjoyed the challenge.
   - ☐ b. feared for their own sons.
   - ☐ c. left the marketplace immediately.

10. Gessler's two servants
    - ☐ a. were as cruel as their master.
    - ☐ b. had confidence in the boy's courage.
    - ☐ c. tried to be kind.

Annette's father had been to a neighboring town on business with Mr. Tinman. He knocked at her door at midnight, and she, in dread, stepped out to him trembling. He was alone. She thought herself the most childish of mortals in supposing that she could have been summoned at midnight to declare her sentiments, and hardly noticed his gloomy depression. He asked her to give him five minutes, then asked her for a kiss, and told her to go to bed and sleep. But Annette would not be sent to sleep. She promised to listen patiently, to bear anything, to be brave. "Is it bad news from home?" she said, speaking of the old home where she had not left her heart, and where his money was invested.

"It's this, my dear Netty," said Van Diemen, suffering her to lead him into her sitting room. "We shall have to leave England."

"Then we are ruined."

"We're not—the rascal can't do that. We might be off to the Continent, or we might go to America—we've money. But we can't stay here. I'll not live at any man's mercy."

"The Continent! America!" exclaimed the enthusiast for England. "Oh, papa, you love living in England so!"

"Not so much as all that, my dear. You do, that I know. But I don't see how it's to be managed. Mart Tinman and I have been at tooth and claw today and half the night, and he has thrown off the mask, or he's dashed something from my sight; I don't know which. I knocked him down."

"Papa!"

"I picked him up."

"Oh," cried Annette, "has Mr. Tinman been hurt?"

"He called me a deserter!"

Annette shuddered.

She did not know what this thing was, but the name of it opened a cabinet of horrors, and she touched her father timidly, to assure him of her constant love, and a little to reassure herself of his substantial identity.

"And I am one," Van Diemen made the confession at the pitch of his voice. "I am a deserter—I'm liable to be branded on the back. And it's in Mart Tinman's power to have me marched away tomorrow morning in the sight of Crikswich, and all I can say for myself, as a man and a Briton, is, I did not desert before the enemy. That I swear I never would have done."

Recalling Facts

1. When Annette's father knocked on her door, he was
   - ☐ a. with Mr. Tinman.
   - ☐ b. trembling.
   - ☐ c. alone.

2. Van Diemen told his daughter that they
   - ☐ a. would soon be happy.
   - ☐ b. would have to leave England.
   - ☐ c. had lost all their money.

3. Van Diemen knocked down
   - ☐ a. Mart Tinman.
   - ☐ b. his daughter.
   - ☐ c. Crikswich.

4. Mr. Tinman called Annette's father a
   - ☐ a. crook.
   - ☐ b. murderer.
   - ☐ c. deserter.

5. Van Diemen said
   - ☐ a. he was a deserter.
   - ☐ b. he did not desert before the enemy.
   - ☐ c. both a and b.

Understanding the Passage

6. Annette greeted the knock on the door with
   - ☐ a. joy.
   - ☐ b. quiet fear.
   - ☐ c. eagerness.

7. Van Diemen did not want to
   - ☐ a. tell his daughter the truth.
   - ☐ b. upset his daughter.
   - ☐ c. fight with Mr. Tinman.

8. The "rascal" refers to
   - ☐ a. Mr. Tinman.
   - ☐ b. Crikswich.
   - ☐ c. Van Diemen.

9. Annette
   - ☐ a. did not like people in America.
   - ☐ b. wanted to go to the Continent.
   - ☐ c. loved England a great deal.

10. Deserters were
    - ☐ a. expelled from the military.
    - ☐ b. treated very harshly.
    - ☐ c. stripped of all their property.

Then Miss Watson she took me in the closet and prayed, but nothing come of it. She told me to pray every day, and whatever I asked for I would get it. But it warn't so. I tried it. Once I got a fish line, but no hooks. It warn't any good to me without hooks. I tried for the hooks three or four times, but somehow I couldn't make it work. By and by, one day, I asked Miss Watson to try for me, but she said I was a fool. She never told me why, and I couldn't make it out no way.

I set down one time back in the woods, and had a long think about it. I says to myself, if a body can get anything they pray for, why don't Deacon Winn get back the money he lost on pork? Why can't the widow get back her silver snuffbox that was stole? Why can't Miss Watson fat up? No, says I to myself, there ain't nothing in it. I went and told the widow about it, and she said the thing a body could get by praying for it was "spiritual gifts." This was too many for me, but she told me what she meant—I must help other people, and do everything I could for other people, and look out for them all the time, and never think about myself. This was including Miss Watson, as I took it. I went out in the woods and turned it over in my mind a long time, but I couldn't see no advantage about it—except for the other people; so at last I reckoned I wouldn't worry about it any more, but just let it go. Sometimes the widow would take me one side and talk about Providence in a way to make a body's mouth water; but maybe next day Miss Watson would take hold and knock it all down again. I judged I could see that there was two Providences, and a poor chap would stand considerable show with the widow's Providence, but if Miss Watson's got him there warn't no help for him any more. I thought it all out, and reckoned I would belong to the widow's if he wanted me, though I couldn't make out how he was a-going to be any better off then than he was before, seeing I was so ignorant.

Recalling Facts

1. Miss Watson took the narrator into the closet to
   - ☐ a. punish him.
   - ☐ b. pack.
   - ☐ c. pray.

2. The narrator once got a fish line but no
   - ☐ a. hooks.
   - ☐ b. bait.
   - ☐ c. pole.

3. Deacon Winn lost his money on
   - ☐ a. silver.
   - ☐ b. the horse races.
   - ☐ c. pork.

4. Someone stole the widow's
   - ☐ a. empty purse.
   - ☐ b. silver snuffbox.
   - ☐ c. personal bible.

5. The narrator decided that there
   - ☐ a. was no heaven.
   - ☐ b. were three Providences.
   - ☐ c. were two Providences.

Understanding the Passage

6. The narrator did not think that
   - ☐ a. the widow was very smart.
   - ☐ b. prayer worked.
   - ☐ c. Miss Watson was religious.

7. The narrator appears to be
   - ☐ a. a young person.
   - ☐ b. a middle-aged widow.
   - ☐ c. an old man.

8. The widow said that prayer would
   - ☐ a. give you anything you want.
   - ☐ b. help you become closer to God.
   - ☐ c. work only if you prayed hard enough.

9. The narrator concluded that prayer only helped
   - ☐ a. people like himself.
   - ☐ b. those who didn't need it.
   - ☐ c. other people.

10. The widow and Miss Watson agreed
    - ☐ a. on the nature of Providence.
    - ☐ b. that prayer was important.
    - ☐ c. that the author was a fool.

"Merry Christmas, little daughters!" said Mrs. March. "I'm glad you began at once, and hope you will keep on. But I want to say one word before we sit down. Not far away from here lies a poor woman with a little newborn baby. Six children are huddled into one bed to keep from freezing, for they have no fire. There is nothing to eat over there, and the oldest boy came to tell me they were suffering from hunger and cold. My girls, will you give them your breakfast as a Christmas present?"

They were all unusually hungry, having waited nearly an hour, and for a minute no one spoke—only a minute, for Jo exclaimed, "I'm so glad you came before we began!"

"May I go and help carry the things to the poor little children?" asked Beth.

"I shall take the cream and the muffins," added Amy, heroically giving up the articles she most liked.

Meg was already covering the buckwheats, and piling the bread into one big plate.

"I thought you'd do it," said Mrs. March, smiling. "You shall all go and help me. When we come back we will have bread and milk for breakfast, and make it up at dinnertime."

They were soon ready, and the procession set out. Fortunately it was early, and they went through back streets, so few people saw them, and no one laughed at the queer party.

A poor, bare room it was, with broken windows, no fire, ragged bedclothes, a sick mother, wailing baby, and a group of pale, hungry children cuddled under one old quilt, trying to keep warm.

How the big eyes stared and the blue lips smiled as the girls went in!

"It is good angels come to us!" said the poor woman, crying for joy.

"Funny angels in hoods and mittens," said Jo, and set them laughing.

In a few minutes it really did seem as if kind spirits had been at work there. Hannah, who had carried wood, made a fire and stopped up the broken panes with old hats and her own cloak. Mrs. March gave the mother tea and gruel, and comforted her with promises of help, while she dressed the little baby as tenderly as if it had been her own. The girls meantime spread the table, set the children round the fire, and fed them like so many hungry birds.

Recalling Facts

1. When Mrs. March came in,
   the girls were getting ready to
   □ a. go to church.
   □ b. eat breakfast.
   □ c. visit friends.

2. Mrs. March asked the girls to
   □ a. give their breakfast to a
      poor family.
   □ b. join her in singing
      Christmas carols.
   □ c. hurry up and finish
      their meal.

3. The girls took their poor
   neighbors
   □ a. muffins and buckwheats.
   □ b. wood for a fire.
   □ c. both a and b.

4. The six poor children slept in
   one bed in order to
   □ a. stay warm.
   □ b. talk to each other during
      the night.
   □ c. make more space for the
      Christmas tree.

5. Mrs. March gave the sick
   woman
   □ a. money.
   □ b. the name of a good
      doctor.
   □ c. tea and gruel.

Understanding the Passage

6. Mrs. March wanted her
   daughters to
   □ a. get married at an
      early age.
   □ b. help people in need.
   □ c. attend college.

7. The poor woman was
   □ a. annoyed with
      Mrs. March.
   □ b. grateful for Mrs. March's
      help.
   □ c. too sick to notice
      Mrs. March.

8. The March family had
   □ a. no home of
      their own.
   □ b. plenty of food.
   □ c. once been to their
      neighbors.

9. The poor woman had
   no fire in the fireplace
   because she
   □ a. had no wood.
   □ b. was afraid of burning
      down the house.
   □ c. liked cold air.

10. When the girls agreed to
    help their neighbors,
    Mrs. March was
    □ a. pleased.
    □ b. disappointed.
    □ c. surprised.

41 *from* **Nevada: a Romance of the West** *by Zane Grey*

It was a cold, bleak November day when Nevada rode into Lineville. Dust and leaves whipped up with the wind. Columns of blue wood smoke curled from the shacks and huts of the straggling hamlet. Part of these habitations, those on one side of the road, lay in California, and those on the other belonged to the state of Nevada. Many a bullet had been fired from one state to kill a man in the other.

Lineville had been a mining town of some pretensions during the early days of the gold rush. Deserted and weathered shacks were mute reminders of more populous times. High on the bleak drab foothill stood the ruins of an ore mill, with long chutes and rusted pipes running down to the stream. Black holes in the cliffs opposite attested to bygone activity of prospectors. Gold was still to be mined in the rugged hills, though only in scant quantity. Prospectors arrived in Lineville, wandered around for a season, then left on their endless search, while other prospectors came. When Nevada had last been there it was possible to find a few honest men and women, but the percentage in the three hundred population was small.

Nevada halted before a gray cabin set well back in a large plot of ground just inside the limits of the town. The place had not changed. A brown swayback horse, with the wind ruffling his deep fuzzy coat, huddled in the lee of an old squat barn. Nevada knew the horse. Corrals and sheds stood farther back at the foot of the rocky slope. Briers and brush surrounded a garden where some late greens showed bright against the red dug up soil. Nevada remembered the rudely painted sign that had been nailed slantwise on the gatepost: Lodgings.

Dismounting, Nevada left his horse and entered, to go round to the back of the cabin. A wide low porch had been stacked to the roof with cut stove wood, handy to the door. Nevada hesitated a moment, then knocked. He heard a bustling inside, brisk footsteps, after which the door was opened by a buxom matron, with ruddy face, big frank eyes, and hair beginning to turn gray.

"Howdy, Mrs. Wood!" he greeted her.

The woman stared, then burst out: "Well, for goodness sake, if it ain't Jim Lacy!"

"I reckon. Are you goin' to ask me in? I'm about froze."

Recalling Facts

1. Lineville was described as a
   - ☐ a. bustling town.
   - ☐ b. boom town.
   - ☐ c. straggling hamlet.

2. Lineville was located on the border of Nevada and
   - ☐ a. Utah.
   - ☐ b. Arizona.
   - ☐ c. California.

3. The population of Lineville was
   - ☐ a. 300.
   - ☐ b. 600.
   - ☐ c. 5,000.

4. The painted sign on the gatepost read:
   - ☐ a. Horses for Sale.
   - ☐ b. Help Wanted.
   - ☐ c. Lodgings.

5. Mrs. Wood
   - ☐ a. recognized Nevada.
   - ☐ b. had never seen Nevada before.
   - ☐ c. was Nevada's mother.

Understanding the Passage

6. Lineville
   - ☐ a. had seen better days.
   - ☐ b. was growing rapidly.
   - ☐ c. once had a railroad.

7. Lineville had seen its fair share of
   - ☐ a. cattle rustlers.
   - ☐ b. stagecoach robbers.
   - ☐ c. gunfighters.

8. Prospectors left Lineville because there
   - ☐ a. wasn't much gold there.
   - ☐ b. were too many killings.
   - ☐ c. both a and b.

9. The people of Lineville are pictured as
   - ☐ a. prosperous and hard working.
   - ☐ b. dishonest drifters.
   - ☐ c. timid and shy.

10. Mrs. Wood appeared to be
    - ☐ a. suspicious.
    - ☐ b. friendly.
    - ☐ c. cold and formal.

One day, after the noon recess, they were marshaled by the teachers—all of the children in the three upper grades—and marched upstairs to the big assembly hall. Eugene and the other children were excited and gossiped in low voices as they went. They had never been called upstairs at this hour. Quite often the bells rang in the halls: they sprang quickly into line and were marched out in double files. That was a fire drill. They liked that. Once they emptied the building in four minutes.

This was something new. They marched into the big room and sat down in blocks of seats assigned to each class: they sat with a seat between each of them. In a moment the door of the principal's office on the left—where little boys were beaten—was opened, and the principal came out. He walked around the corner of the big room and stepped softly up on the platform. He began to talk.

He was a new principal. Young Armstrong was gone. The new principal was older. He was about thirty-eight years old. He was a strong, rather heavy man a little under six feet tall; he was one of a large family who had grown up on a Tennessee farm. His father was poor but he had helped his children to get an education. All this Eugene knew already, because the principal made long talks to them in the morning and said he had never had their advantages. He pointed to himself with some pride. And he urged the little boys, playfully but earnestly, to "be not like dumb driven cattle, be a hero in the strife." That was poetry, Longfellow.

The principal had thick powerful shoulders; clumsy white arms, knotted with big awkward country muscles. Eugene had seen him once hoeing in the schoolyard; each of them had been given a plant to set out. He got those muscles on the farm. The boys said he beat very hard. He walked with a clumsy stealthy tread—awkward and comical enough, it is true, but he could be up at a boy's back before you knew it.

He had a white face, with deep flat cheeks, a pallid nose, a trifle deeper in its color than his face, and a thin slightly bowed mouth. His hair was coarse, black, and thick, but he never let it grow too long.

Recalling Facts

1. The fastest fire drill lasted just
   - ☐ a. two minutes.
   - ☐ b. four minutes.
   - ☐ c. six minutes.

2. In the big room, the children sat according to
   - ☐ a. age.
   - ☐ b. sex.
   - ☐ c. class.

3. The new principal
   - ☐ a. grew up on a farm.
   - ☐ b. was younger than Armstrong.
   - ☐ c. was very fat.

4. The new principal quoted
   - ☐ a. Lincoln.
   - ☐ b. Armstrong.
   - ☐ c. Longfellow.

5. Eugene was a
   - ☐ a. teacher.
   - ☐ b. student.
   - ☐ c. parent.

Understanding the Passage

6. Calling the children upstairs to the assembly hall was
   - ☐ a. routine.
   - ☐ b. very unusual.
   - ☐ c. done after fire drills.

7. This school believed in
   - ☐ a. spiritual development.
   - ☐ b. job training.
   - ☐ c. physical punishment.

8. The new principal
   - ☐ a. overcame his poor background.
   - ☐ b. was a member of the upper class.
   - ☐ c. wrote daily in a journal.

9. Eugene was most impressed by the new principal's
   - ☐ a. speaking ability.
   - ☐ b. coarse black hair.
   - ☐ c. physical strength.

10. The principal considered Eugene and his friends
    - ☐ a. lucky to have the chance for an education.
    - ☐ b. unable to learn difficult formulas.
    - ☐ c. smarter than children back in Tennessee.

Nadyezhda Filippovna looked indifferently at her mother and began walking up and down the room.

"The barometer was rising yesterday," she said doubtfully, "but they say it is falling again today."

The old lady laid out the cards in three long rows and shook her head.

"Do you miss him?" she asked, glancing at her daughter.

"Of course."

"I see you do. I should think so. He hasn't been here for five days. In May the utmost was two, or at most three days, and now it is serious, five days! I am not his wife, and yet I miss him. And yesterday, when I heard the barometer was rising, I ordered them to kill a chicken and prepare a carp for Alexey Stepanovitch. He likes them."

"My heart aches for him," said the daughter. "We are dull, but it is duller still for him, you know, mamma."

"I should think so! In the lawcourts day in and day out, and in the empty flat at night alone like an owl."

"And what is so awful, mamma, he is alone there without servants; there is no one to set the urn or bring him water. Why didn't he engage a valet for the summer months? And what use is the summer villa at all if he does not care for it? I told him there was no need to have it, but no, 'It is for the sake of your health,' he said, and what is wrong with my health? It makes me ill that he should have to put up with so much on my account."

Looking over her mother's shoulder, the daughter noticed a mistake in the cards, bent down to the table and began correcting them. A silence followed. Both looked at the cards and imagined how their Alexey Stepanovitch, utterly forlorn, was sitting now in the town in his gloomy, empty study and working, hungry, exhausted, yearning for his family.

"Do you know what, mamma?" said Nadyezhda Filippovna suddenly, and her eyes began to shine. "If the weather is the same tomorrow I'll go by the first train and see him in town! Anyway, I shall find out how he is, have a look at him, and pour out his tea."

And both of them began to wonder how it was that this idea, so simple and easy to carry out, had not occurred to them before.

Recalling Facts

1. Yesterday the barometer was
   - ☐ a. rising.
   - ☐ b. steady.
   - ☐ c. falling.

2. The old lady asked her daughter if she missed
   - ☐ a. Alexey.
   - ☐ b. dinner.
   - ☐ c. the train.

3. The old lady had prepared a
   - ☐ a. steak for Alexey.
   - ☐ b. cup of tea for Alexey.
   - ☐ c. carp for Alexey.

4. Alexey was alone
   - ☐ a. at the summer villa.
   - ☐ b. in his town study.
   - ☐ c. at the railroad station.

5. The next day Nadyezhda planned to visit Alexey by
   - ☐ a. boat.
   - ☐ b. train.
   - ☐ c. wagon.

Understanding the Passage

6. Alexey was often
   - ☐ a. gone for two or three days.
   - ☐ b. seen playing cards.
   - ☐ c. upset with his wife and mother-in-law.

7. The two women thought that Alexey must be
   - ☐ a. enjoying life in town.
   - ☐ b. thinking about the weather.
   - ☐ c. sad and lonely.

8. Apparently, Alexey's work had something to do with
   - ☐ a. the stock market.
   - ☐ b. the law.
   - ☐ c. entertaining.

9. Alexey seemed to be a
   - ☐ a. caring man.
   - ☐ b. troublesome man.
   - ☐ c. forgetful man.

10. Nadyezhda's suggestion to visit Alexey
    - ☐ a. had already occurred to her mother.
    - ☐ b. puzzled her mother.
    - ☐ c. pleased her mother.

This story is slightly immoral. It concerns Harry Hart, whose frankness endeared him to fellow members of the Friars' Club. Music writers have never been noted for self-loathing and Harry was a refreshing exception to the general run. That was before *Upsy Daisy* began its year's tenancy of the Casino.

You can judge what sort of person he was by listening in on a talk he had at the club one night with Sam Rose, lyricist of "Nora's Nightie," "Sheila's Shirt" and a hundred popular songs. They were sitting alone at the table nearest the senile piano.

"Sam," said Harry, "I was wondering if there's a chance of you and I getting together."

"What's happened to Kane?" asked Sam.

"It's off between he and I," Harry replied. "That dame ruined him. I guess she married him to make an honest man of him. Anyways, he got so honest that I couldn't stand it no more. You know how I am, Sam—live and let live. I don't question nobody's ethics or whatever you call them, as long as they don't question mine. We're all trying to get along; that's the way I look at it. At that, I've heard better lyrics than he wrote for those two rhythm numbers of mine in *Lottie*; in fact, between you and I, I thought he made a bum out of those two numbers. They sold like hymns, so I was really able to bear up when we reached the parting of the ways."

"But I'll tell you the climax just to show you how silly a guy can get. You remember our 'Yes, Yes, Eulalie.' Well, they made a spot for a swell love duet near the end of the first act and I had a tune for it that was a smash. You know I'm not bragging when I say that; I don't claim it as my tune, but it was and is a smash. I mean the 'Catch Me' number."

"I'll say it's a smash!" agreed Sam.

"But a smash in spite of the words," said Harry.

"You're right," said Sam.

"Well, the first time I played this tune for him, he went nuts over it and I gave him a lead sheet and he showed it to his wife. It seems she plays piano a little and she played this melody and she told him I had stole it from some opera."

Recalling Facts

1. The members of the Friars' Club enjoyed Harry's
   - ☐ a. jokes.
   - ☐ b. frankness.
   - ☐ c. generosity.

2. Harry was
   - ☐ a. an actor.
   - ☐ b. a theater owner.
   - ☐ c. a song writer.

3. Sam Rose wrote the words to
   - ☐ a. "Sheila's Shirt."
   - ☐ b. *Upsy Daisy*.
   - ☐ c. *Lottie*.

4. Kane and Harry were
   - ☐ a. in love with the same woman.
   - ☐ b. once musical partners.
   - ☐ c. a song and dance team.

5. Kane's wife
   - ☐ a. played the piano a little.
   - ☐ b. wrote an opera.
   - ☐ c. sang in *Catch Me* at the Casino.

Understanding the Passage

6. Most music writers
   - ☐ a. make lots of money.
   - ☐ b. think highly of themselves.
   - ☐ c. marry piano players.

7. Apparently, *Upsy Daisy* was
   - ☐ a. a big failure.
   - ☐ b. a fair success.
   - ☐ c. stolen from an opera.

8. Harry blamed his split with Kane on
   - ☐ a. himself.
   - ☐ b. Sam Rose.
   - ☐ c. Kane's wife.

9. Harry thought that Kane's lyrics were
   - ☐ a. not very good.
   - ☐ b. inspiring.
   - ☐ c. too romantic.

10. Harry liked to think of himself as
    - ☐ a. a mean person.
    - ☐ b. an easygoing person.
    - ☐ c. a suspicious person.

The moment for closing the trial had arrived. The President ordered the prisoner to stand up and asked him the usual question. "Have you anything to add to your defense?" The man, who was rolling in his hands his hideous cap, made no reply, and the President repeated his question. This time the man heard and seemed to understand. He moved like a person who is waking up, looked around him at the public, his counsel, the jury, and the court, laid his monstrous fist on the woodwork in front of his bench, and, suddenly fixing his eyes on the public prosecutor, began to speak. It was an eruption; from the way in which the words escaped from his lips, all scrambled and pell-mell, it seemed as if they were all striving to get out at the same time. He said:

"I have this to say. I was a wheelright in Paris, and worked for Master Baloup. It is a hard trade, is a wheelwright's; you always work in the open air, in yards, under sheds when you have a good master, but never in a room, because you want space, look you. In winter you are so cold that you swing your arms to warm you, but the masters don't like that, for they say it wastes time. Handling iron when there is ice between the stones is rough work; it soon uses a man up. You are old when quite young in that trade. At forty a man is finished. I was fifty-three and had hard lines of it. And then the workmen are so unkind. When a man is not so young as he was, they call him an old fool, an old brute! I only earned thirty sous a day, for the masters took advantage of my age and paid me as little as they could. With that I had my daughter, who was a washerwoman in the river. She earned a little for her part, and the pair of us managed to live. She was bothered too. All day in a tub up to your waist, in the snow and rain, and with the wind that cuts your face. When it freezes it is all the same, for you must wash; there are persons who have not much linen and expect it home. If a woman did not wash, she would lose her customers."

Recalling Facts

1. The prisoner fixed his eyes on the
   - ☐ a. bench.
   - ☐ b. group of jurors.
   - ☐ c. public prosecutor.

2. Master Baloup was the prisoner's
   - ☐ a. father.
   - ☐ b. boss.
   - ☐ c. counsel.

3. According to the prisoner, a man was finished as a wheelwright by age
   - ☐ a. forty.
   - ☐ b. fifty.
   - ☐ c. sixty.

4. The prisoner earned
   - ☐ a. ten sous a day.
   - ☐ b. thirty sous a day.
   - ☐ c. one hundred sous a day.

5. The prisoner's daughter worked as a
   - ☐ a. kitchen helper.
   - ☐ b. housemaid.
   - ☐ c. washerwoman.

Understanding the Passage

6. The prisoner was not an experienced
   - ☐ a. wheelwright.
   - ☐ b. public speaker.
   - ☐ c. both a and b.

7. The wheelwright masters
   - ☐ a. appreciated and rewarded good work.
   - ☐ b. demanded constant work of their employees.
   - ☐ c. paid their employees excellent wages.

8. Compared to other wheelwrights, the prisoner was
   - ☐ a. young.
   - ☐ b. of equal age.
   - ☐ c. old.

9. The prisoner did not appear to have much choice in his
   - ☐ a. working conditions.
   - ☐ b. wages.
   - ☐ c. both a and b.

10. Apparently, the prisoner's daughter
    - ☐ a. had been separated from her father.
    - ☐ b. worked just as hard as the prisoner.
    - ☐ c. testified against her father.

I was handling a visiting card inscribed: "Rev. Ellis Shorter," and underneath was written in pencil, "Asking the favor of a few moments' conversation on a most urgent matter."

I quickly put my tie on, and then hurried into the drawing room. The Reverend rose at my entrance, flapping like a seal. He flapped a plaid shawl over his right arm; he flapped a pair of pathetic black gloves; he flapped his clothes. I may say, without exaggeration, that he flapped his eyelids, as he rose. He was a bald-browed, white-whiskered old clergyman of a flappy and floppy type. He said:

"I am so sorry. I am so very sorry. I am so extremely sorry. I come—I can only say—I can only say in my defense, that I come—upon an important matter. Pray forgive me."

I told him I forgave perfectly and waited.

"What I have to say," he said, brokenly, "is so dreadful—it is so dreadful—I have lived a quiet life."

I was burning to get away, for it was already doubtful if I should be in time for dinner. But there was something about the old man's honest air of bitterness that seemed to open to me the possibilities of life larger and more tragic than my own.

I said, gently: "Pray go on."

Nevertheless, the old gentleman, being a gentleman as well as old, noticed my secret impatience and seemed still more unmanned.

"I'm so sorry," he said, weakly, "I wouldn't have come—but for—your friend, Major Brown, recommended me to come here."

"Major Brown!" I said, with some interest.

"Yes," said the Reverend Mr. Shorter, feverishly, flapping his plaid shawl about. "He told me you helped him in a great difficulty—and my difficulty! Oh, my dear sir, it's a matter of life and death."

I rose abruptly, in an acute perplexity. "Will it take long, Mr. Shorter?" I asked. "I have to go out to dinner almost at once."

He rose also, trembling from head to foot, and yet somehow, with all his moral palsy, he rose to the dignity of his age and his office.

"I have no right, Mr. Swinburne—I have no right at all," he said. "If you have to go out to dinner, you have, of course—a perfect right—of course, a perfect right. But when you come back—a man will be dead."

Recalling Facts

1. Reverend Ellis Shorter had
   - ☐ a. a bald head and a black beard.
   - ☐ b. white gloves and a white shawl.
   - ☐ c. white whiskers and black gloves.

2. The Reverend claimed that he had lived a
   - ☐ a. quiet life.
   - ☐ b. sinful life.
   - ☐ c. dangerous life.

3. The narrator was on his way to
   - ☐ a. dinner.
   - ☐ b. the theater.
   - ☐ c. the library.

4. Major Brown had recommended that the Reverend
   - ☐ a. leave town.
   - ☐ b. call on the narrator.
   - ☐ c. give up hope.

5. Mr. Swinburne was
   - ☐ a. the narrator.
   - ☐ b. Major Brown's real name.
   - ☐ c. the man who would be dead.

Understanding the Passage

6. The Reverend appeared to be
   - ☐ a. very apologetic.
   - ☐ b. self-confident.
   - ☐ c. very impatient.

7. The narrator was
   - ☐ a. in a hurry.
   - ☐ b. sleepy.
   - ☐ c. embarrassed.

8. The Reverend believed that what he had to say was
   - ☐ a. very important.
   - ☐ b. of little interest.
   - ☐ c. hard to believe.

9. The Reverend seemed to
   - ☐ a. sense the narrator's impatience.
   - ☐ b. be angry with the narrator.
   - ☐ c. have given up all hope for help.

10. The Reverend tried to be
    - ☐ a. polite.
    - ☐ b. rude.
    - ☐ c. brief.

Millie stood leaning against the verandah until the men were out of sight. When they were far down the road Willie Cox turned round on his horse and waved, but she didn't wave back. She nodded her head a little and made a grimace. Not a bad young fellow, Willie Cox, but a bit too free and easy for her taste. Oh, my word! it was hot. Enough to fry your hair!

Millie put her handkerchief over her head and shaded her eyes with her hand. In the distance along the dusty road she could see the horses, like brown spots dancing up and down, and when she looked away from them and over the burnt paddocks she could see them still—just before her eyes, jumping like mosquitoes. It was half-past two in the afternoon. The sun hung in the faded blue sky like a burning mirror, and away beyond the paddocks the blue mountains quivered and leapt like sea.

Sid wouldn't be back until half-past ten. He had ridden over to the township with four of the boys to help hunt down the young fellow who'd murdered Mr. Williamson. Such a dreadful thing! And Mrs. Williamson left all alone with those kids. Funny! She couldn't think of Mr. Williamson being dead! He was such a one for a joke. Always having a lark. Willie Cox said they found him in the barn, shot bang through the head, and the young English "johnny" who'd been on the station learning farming—disappeared. Funny! She couldn't think of anyone shooting Mr. Williamson, and him so popular and all. My word! When they caught that young man! Well, you couldn't be sorry for a young fellow like that. As Sid said, if he wasn't strung up where would they all be? A man like that doesn't stop at one go.

Millie went back into the kitchen. She put some ashes on the stove and sprinkled them with water. Languidly, the sweat pouring down her face, and dropping off her nose and chin, she cleared away the dinner, and going into the bedroom, stared at herself in the fly-specked mirror, and wiped her face and neck with a towel. She didn't know what was the matter with herself that afternoon. She could have a good cry—just for nothing—and then change her blouse and have a good cup of tea. Yes, she felt like that!

Recalling Facts

1. When Willie Cox turned and waved, Millie
   - ☐ a. blew him a kiss.
   - ☐ b. waved back.
   - ☐ c. nodded her head a little.

2. The weather was
   - ☐ a. cold.
   - ☐ b. rainy.
   - ☐ c. hot.

3. This scene took place
   - ☐ a. in the early morning.
   - ☐ b. in the afternoon.
   - ☐ c. just after supper.

4. The murder victim was
   - ☐ a. Mr. Williamson.
   - ☐ b. Willie Cox.
   - ☐ c. a young English "johnny."

5. Millie's fly-specked mirror was located in the
   - ☐ a. kitchen.
   - ☐ b. bedroom.
   - ☐ c. bathroom.

Understanding the Passage

6. Millie showed
   - ☐ a. great interest in Willie Cox.
   - ☐ b. only slight interest in Willie Cox.
   - ☐ c. no interest whatsoever in Willie Cox.

7. From her position, Millie enjoyed
   - ☐ a. cool shade.
   - ☐ b. a long view.
   - ☐ c. a moist breeze.

8. Everyone seemed to know
   - ☐ a. the identity of the murderer.
   - ☐ b. how to help Mrs. Williamson.
   - ☐ c. when the posse would return.

9. Millie had trouble thinking about
   - ☐ a. Willie Cox's attention.
   - ☐ b. the young English "johnny."
   - ☐ c. the death of someone she knew.

10. To Millie, Willie Cox appeared to be
    - ☐ a. cool and sophisticated.
    - ☐ b. unadventurous.
    - ☐ c. a bit crude.

On January 17, Utterson betook himself to Dr. Lanyon's. He was not denied admittance; but when he came in, he was shocked at the change which had taken place in the doctor's appearance. He had his death warrant written legibly upon his face. The rosy man had grown pale; his flesh had fallen away; he was visibly balder and older. And yet it was not so much these tokens of a swift physical decay that arrested the lawyer's notice, as a look in the eye and quality of manner that seemed to testify to some deep-seated terror of the mind. It was unlikely that the doctor should fear death; and yet that was what Utterson was tempted to suspect. "Yes," he thought; "he is a doctor, he must know his own state and that his days are counted; and the knowledge is more than he can bear." And yet when Utterson remarked on his ill-looks, it was with an air of great firmness that Lanyon declared himself a doomed man.

"I have had a shock," he said, "and I shall never recover. It is a question of weeks. Well, life has been pleasant; I liked it; yes, sir, I used to like it. I sometimes think if we knew all, we should be more glad to get away."

"Jekyll is ill, too," observed Utterson. "Have you seen him?"

But Lanyon's face changed, and he held up a trembling hand. "I wish to see or hear no more of Dr. Jekyll," he said in a loud, unsteady voice. "I am quite done with that person; and I beg that you will spare me any allusion to one whom I regard as dead."

"Tut-tut," said Mr. Utterson; and then after a considerable pause, "Can't I do anything?" he inquired. "We are three very old friends, Lanyon; we shall not live to make others."

"Nothing can be done," returned Lanyon; "ask himself."

"He will not see me," said the lawyer.

"I am not surprised at that," was the reply. "Someday, Utterson, after I am dead, you may perhaps come to learn the right and wrong of this. I cannot tell you. And in the meantime, if you can sit and talk with me of other things, for God's sake, stay and do so. But if you cannot keep clear of this accursed topic, then in God's name, go, for I cannot bear it."

Recalling Facts

1. Utterson was struck by
   Dr. Lanyon's
   - □ a. unhealthy appearance.
   - □ b. happiness.
   - □ c. cheerful attitude.

2. Lanyon believed he was
   - □ a. dying.
   - □ b. about to achieve a
     breakthrough.
   - □ c. Jekyll's best friend.

3. Lanyon felt his life had been
   - □ a. wasted.
   - □ b. misspent.
   - □ c. pleasant.

4. Utterson was an old friend of
   - □ a. Lanyon's.
   - □ b. Jekyll's.
   - □ c. both a and b.

5. Lanyon asked the doctor not
   to mention
   - □ a. death.
   - □ b. Jekyll.
   - □ c. the subject of science.

Understanding the Passage

6. Until recently, Lanyon
   had been
   - □ a. out of the country.
   - □ b. reasonably healthy.
   - □ c. living with Utterson.

7. Utterson was a
   - □ a. doctor.
   - □ b. lawyer.
   - □ c. scientist.

8. Lanyon believed he was
   dying as a result of a
   - □ a. terrible shock he
     had had.
   - □ b. blow to the head.
   - □ c. medicine Dr. Jekyll had
     given him.

9. Utterson wanted Lanyon to
   - □ a. end his quarrel
     with Jekyll.
   - □ b. see a new doctor.
   - □ c. move his laboratory.

10. Utterson's motive was to
    - □ a. hurt Jekyll.
    - □ b. help Lanyon.
    - □ c. both a and b.

Yes, that was little Tuk. His name was not really Tuk. But when he could not speak plainly, he used to call himself so. It was to mean "Charley;" and it does very well if one only knows it. Now, he was to take care of his little sister Gustava, who was much smaller than he, and at the same time he was to learn his lesson; but these two things would not suit well together. The poor boy sat there with his little sister on his lap, and sang her all kinds of songs that he knew, and every now and then he gave a glance at the geography book that lay open before him; by tomorrow morning he was to know all the towns in Zealand by heart.

His mother then came home. She took little Gustava in her arms. Tuk ran quickly to the window, and read so zealously that he almost read his eyes out, for it became darker and darker. His mother had no money to buy candles.

"There goes the old washerwoman," said his mother, as she looked out of the window. "The poor woman has to carry the pail of water from the well. Be a good boy, Tuk, and run across, and help the old woman. Won't you?"

And Tuk ran across quickly, and helped her; but when he came back into the room it had become quite dark. There was nothing said about a candle, and now he had to go to bed, and his bed was an old settle. There he lay, and thought of his geography lesson, and of Zealand, and of all the master had said. He ought certainly to have read it again, but he could not do that. So he put the geography book under his pillow, because he had heard that this is a very good way to learn one's lesson; but one cannot depend upon it. There he lay, and thought and thought; and all at once he fancied someone kissed him upon his eyes and mouth. He slept, and yet he did not sleep. It was just as if the old washerwoman were looking at his with her kind eyes, and saying—

"It would be a great pity if you did not know your lesson tomorrow. You have helped me, therefore now I will help you. And Providence will help us both."

Recalling Facts

1. Tuk entertained Gustava by
   - ☐ a. reading stories.
   - ☐ b. singing songs.
   - ☐ c. standing on his head.

2. Tuk was supposed to
   be studying
   - ☐ a. geography.
   - ☐ b. history.
   - ☐ c. science.

3. To read, Tuk had to
   depend on
   - ☐ a. an oil lamp.
   - ☐ b. candlelight.
   - ☐ c. sunlight.

4. Tuk helped the washer-
   woman carry
   - ☐ a. her laundry.
   - ☐ b. a pail of water.
   - ☐ c. her groceries.

5. After dark, Tuk put his
   textbook
   - ☐ a. on his desk.
   - ☐ b. with his toys.
   - ☐ c. under his pillow.

Understanding the Passage

6. Tuk's family had
   - ☐ a. little money.
   - ☐ b. few friends.
   - ☐ c. no place to live.

7. Tuk wanted to
   - ☐ a. ignore his sister.
   - ☐ b. do well in school.
   - ☐ c. avoid the
     washerwoman.

8. Tuk appeared to be
   - ☐ a. hard to discipline.
   - ☐ b. a rather slow learner.
   - ☐ c. an obedient child.

9. Tuk could best be
   described as
   - ☐ a. earnest and unselfish.
   - ☐ b. quiet and lonely.
   - ☐ c. cruel and vicious.

10. At the end of the passage,
    Tuk appeared to be
    - ☐ a. studying.
    - ☐ b. dreaming.
    - ☐ c. crying.

Morrison didn't understand. This was one of those things that don't happen. He had no real inkling of what it meant, till Heyst said:

"I can lend you the amount."

"You have the money?" whispered Morrison. "Do you mean here, in your pocket?"

"Yes, on me. Glad to be of use."

"Miracles do happen," thought Morrison. To him, as to all of us in the islands, this wandering Heyst, who didn't toil or spin visibly, seemed the very last person to be the agent of Providence in an affair concerned with money. That he should carry a sum of money in his pocket seemed somehow inconceivable.

So inconceivable that as they were trudging together through the sand of the roadway to the customhouse—another mud hovel—to pay the fine, Morrison broke into a cold sweat, stopped short, and exclaimed in faltering accents, "I say! You aren't joking, Heyst?"

"Joking!" Heyst's blue eyes went hard as he turned them on Morrison. "In what way, may I ask?" he continued with strict politeness.

Morrison was abashed. "Forgive me, Heyst. You must have been sent by God in answer to my prayer. But I have been nearly off my chump for three days with worry; and it suddenly struck me: 'What if it's the Devil who has sent him?' "

"I have no connection with the supernatural," said Heyst graciously, moving on. "Nobody has sent me. I just happened along."

"I know better," contradicted Morrison. "I may be unworthy, but I have been heard. I know it. I feel it. Why should you offer—"

Heyst inclined his head, as from respect for a conviction in which he could not share. But he stuck to his point by muttering that in the presence of an odious fact like this, it was natural.

Later in the day, the fine paid, and the two of them on board the brig, from which the guard had been removed, Morrison—who, besides being a gentleman, was also an honest fellow—began to talk about repayment. He knew very well his inability to lay by any sum of money. It was partly the fault of circumstances and partly of his temperament. It would have been very difficult to split the responsibility between the two. Even Morrison himself could not say.

"I don't know how it is that I've never been able to save. It's some sort of curse."

Recalling Facts

1. Heyst had the money in his
   - ☐ a. checkbook.
   - ☐ b. bank.
   - ☐ c. pocket.

2. Morrison needed the money to
   - ☐ a. pay a fine.
   - ☐ b. buy a train ticket.
   - ☐ c. build a house.

3. Morrison thought that Heyst had been sent by
   - ☐ a. the bank.
   - ☐ b. his long-lost relatives.
   - ☐ c. something supernatural.

4. Morrison was
   - ☐ a. a lonely person.
   - ☐ b. an honest gentleman.
   - ☐ c. a dishonest gambler.

5. Morrison had never been able to
   - ☐ a. tell the truth.
   - ☐ b. save money.
   - ☐ c. make friends.

Understanding the Passage

6. When Heyst offered him the money, Morrison
   - ☐ a. was completely astonished.
   - ☐ b. rudely grabbed it.
   - ☐ c. knew he had to turn him down.

7. Heyst had no
   - ☐ a. feelings for the needy.
   - ☐ b. apparent source of income.
   - ☐ c. proper manners.

8. When Heyst assured him that he wasn't joking, Morrison was
   - ☐ a. outraged.
   - ☐ b. a little ashamed.
   - ☐ c. very disappointed.

9. Heyst answered Morrison's suspicious questions with
   - ☐ a. civilized kindness.
   - ☐ b. sharp rebukes.
   - ☐ c. all-knowing silence.

10. Morrison managed his money
   - ☐ a. very cleverly.
   - ☐ b. as well as most people.
   - ☐ c. quite poorly.

Answer Key

Progress Graph

Pacing Graph

Answer Key

1	1. b	2. a	3. c	4. a	5. c	6. a	7. c	8. b	9. c	10. b
2	1. a	2. a	3. b	4. b	5. b	6. b	7. b	8. b	9. c	10. a
3	1. b	2. a	3. c	4. b	5. c	6. a	7. c	8. a	9. a	10. b
4	1. b	2. a	3. c	4. c	5. b	6. a	7. a	8. b	9. b	10. b
5	1. b	2. c	3. a	4. c	5. a	6. b	7. b	8. a	9. c	10. b
6	1. a	2. b	3. c	4. c	5. b	6. c	7. c	8. a	9. b	10. c
7	1. c	2. a	3. a	4. c	5. b	6. b	7. b	8. a	9. b	10. c
8	1. c	2. a	3. b	4. a	5. a	6. c	7. b	8. a	9. c	10. a
9	1. b	2. b	3. a	4. b	5. a	6. c	7. b	8. b	9. c	10. b
10	1. b	2. b	3. c	4. a	5. b	6. b	7. c	8. c	9. b	10. a
11	1. a	2. b	3. c	4. b	5. c	6. b	7. c	8. b	9. c	10. a
12	1. c	2. a	3. c	4. b	5. c	6. c	7. b	8. b	9. a	10. b
13	1. c	2. b	3. b	4. b	5. a	6. b	7. b	8. a	9. a	10. c
14	1. b	2. c	3. a	4. c	5. a	6. c	7. a	8. a	9. b	10. c
15	1. a	2. a	3. c	4. a	5. a	6. c	7. a	8. c	9. a	10. b
16	1. a	2. b	3. c	4. c	5. c	6. c	7. c	8. a	9. b	10. a
17	1. c	2. a	3. a	4. c	5. b	6. a	7. c	8. c	9. a	10. b
18	1. c	2. b	3. a	4. a	5. c	6. c	7. a	8. b	9. a	10. c
19	1. a	2. a	3. b	4. c	5. c	6. b	7. c	8. c	9. b	10. a
20	1. c	2. b	3. b	4. c	5. b	6. b	7. b	8. c	9. b	10. a
21	1. c	2. b	3. b	4. a	5. b	6. b	7. a	8. b	9. a	10. a
22	1. b	2. b	3. c	4. b	5. a	6. a	7. c	8. a	9. c	10. b
23	1. c	2. a	3. b	4. a	5. b	6. a	7. a	8. b	9. c	10. a
24	1. c	2. b	3. a	4. c	5. a	6. a	7. b	8. c	9. b	10. a
25	1. c	2. c	3. a	4. a	5. b	6. b	7. c	8. c	9. b	10. a

26	1. b	2. c	3. a	4. a	5. b	6. a	7. c	8. b	9. a	10. b
27	1. b	2. a	3. c	4. a	5. a	6. b	7. a	8. c	9. a	10. b
28	1. b	2. a	3. c	4. c	5. a	6. a	7. b	8. c	9. a	10. b
29	1. a	2. a	3. b	4. a	5. c	6. c	7. a	8. b	9. c	10. b
30	1. b	2. a	3. b	4. b	5. c	6. b	7. a	8. a	9. a	10. b
31	1. b	2. a	3. b	4. a	5. c	6. a	7. b	8. a	9. c	10. b
32	1. b	2. c	3. b	4. a	5. a	6. b	7. a	8. c	9. a	10. b
33	1. c	2. c	3. c	4. a	5. b	6. a	7. b	8. c	9. c	10. c
34	1. c	2. b	3. a	4. b	5. a	6. b	7. c	8. a	9. a	10. c
35	1. c	2. b	3. b	4. a	5. b	6. a	7. b	8. a	9. c	10. c
36	1. c	2. a	3. c	4. b	5. b	6. a	7. c	8. b	9. b	10. c
37	1. b	2. c	3. a	4. a	5. c	6. b	7. a	8. c	9. b	10. c
38	1. c	2. b	3. a	4. c	5. c	6. b	7. b	8. a	9. c	10. b
39	1. c	2. a	3. c	4. b	5. c	6. b	7. a	8. b	9. c	10. b
40	1. b	2. a	3. c	4. a	5. c	6. b	7. b	8. b	9. a	10. a
41	1. c	2. c	3. a	4. c	5. a	6. a	7. c	8. a	9. b	10. b
42	1. b	2. c	3. a	4. c	5. b	6. b	7. c	8. a	9. c	10. a
43	1. a	2. a	3. c	4. b	5. b	6. a	7. c	8. b	9. a	10. c
44	1. b	2. c	3. a	4. b	5. a	6. b	7. b	8. c	9. a	10. b
45	1. c	2. b	3. a	4. b	5. c	6. b	7. b	8. c	9. c	10. b
46	1. c	2. a	3. a	4. b	5. a	6. a	7. a	8. a	9. a	10. a
47	1. c	2. c	3. b	4. a	5. b	6. b	7. b	8. a	9. c	10. c
48	1. a	2. a	3. c	4. c	5. b	6. b	7. b	8. a	9. a	10. b
49	1. b	2. a	3. c	4. b	5. c	6. a	7. b	8. c	9. a	10. b
50	1. c	2. a	3. c	4. b	5. b	6. a	7. b	8. b	9. a	10. c

Progress Graph (1–25)

Directions: Write your comprehension score in the box under the selection number. Then put an x on the line above each box to show your reading time and words-per-minute reading rate.

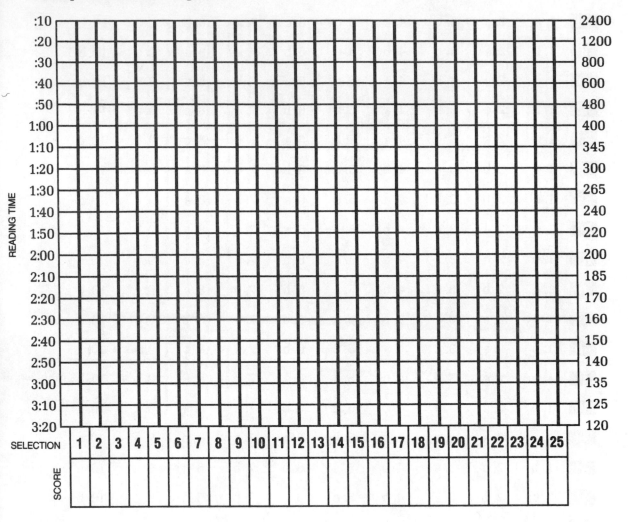

READING TIME																										
:10																										2400
:20																										1200
:30																										800
:40																										600
:50																										480
1:00																										400
1:10																										345
1:20																										300
1:30																										265
1:40																										240
1:50																										220
2:00																										200
2:10																										185
2:20																										170
2:30																										160
2:40																										150
2:50																										140
3:00																										135
3:10																										125
3:20																										120

SELECTION	1	2	3	4	5	6	7	8	9	10	11	12	13	14	15	16	17	18	19	20	21	22	23	24	25
SCORE																										

Progress Graph (26–50)

Directions: Write your comprehension score in the box under the selection number. Then put an x on the line above each box to show your reading time and words-per-minute reading rate.

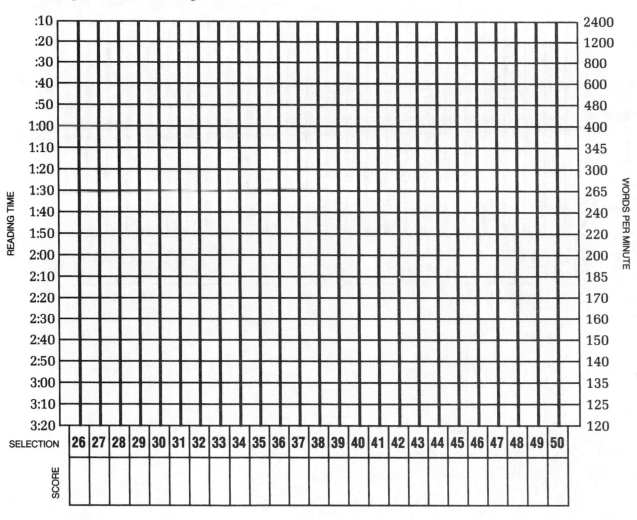

READING TIME		WORDS PER MINUTE
:10		2400
:20		1200
:30		800
:40		600
:50		480
1:00		400
1:10		345
1:20		300
1:30		265
1:40		240
1:50		220
2:00		200
2:10		185
2:20		170
2:30		160
2:40		150
2:50		140
3:00		135
3:10		125
3:20		120

SELECTION: 26 27 28 29 30 31 32 33 34 35 36 37 38 39 40 41 42 43 44 45 46 47 48 49 50

SCORE

Pacing Graph

Directions: In the boxes labeled "Pace" along the bottom of the graph, write your words-per-minute rate. On the vertical line above each box, put an x to indicate your comprehension score.

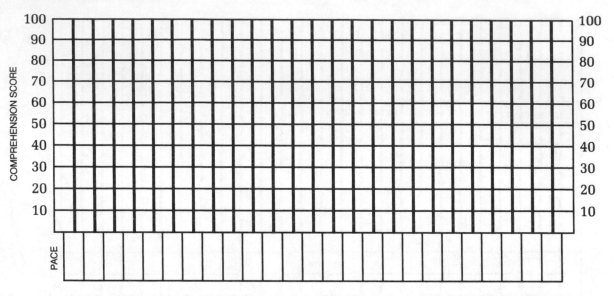